Stop Reacting

and *Start* **Responding**

108 Ways
to Discipline Consciously
and Become the Parent You Want to Be

Sharon Silver, Parent Educator

One Voice Publishing
Giving Your Voice Wings™

Stop Reacting and Start Responding:
108 Ways to Discipline Consciously and Become the Parent
You Want To Be

Book Cover Design: Michelle Radomski with Kerry Turner, One Voice Can

Interior Layout: Joe Radomski with Myra House, One Voice Can

Editing: Off Ramp Publishing and Susie Overholt and Judi Moss

One Voice Can
www.OneVoiceCan.com

Printed in the USA

To order additional copies visit:
www.proactiveparenting.net

ATTENTION: CORPORATIONS, SCHOOLS and
                    LIBRARIES

Stop Reacting and Start Responding is available at quantity discounts, with bulk purchases for schools, corporations, parent networks, and promotional fundraising.

For more information contact Proactive Parenting™ at www.proactiveparenting.net

Praise For This Book:

"A glorious collection of parenting tips that moms can instantly use to help them raise good and caring kids."
Michele Borba, Ed.D,. author of *The Big Book of Parenting Solutions: 101 Answers to Your Everyday Challenges and Wildest Worries*

"In an era when we all feel confused about "how to parent" our children, Parent Educator ~ Sharon Silver, provides sensible, modern advice real parents can really use. Sharon simplifies developmental concepts and provides parents with actionable advice to raise healthy, ethical, competent kids in a flash."
Lynne Kenney, PsyD, Pediatric Psychologist, author of *The Family Coach Method*

"I interview top parenting experts every day for my work, but Sharon Silver stood out to me the very first time I talked to her. Her advice to parents is incredibly calming and very do-able. I especially appreciate that her solutions always include sample conversations parents can use with their kids. Concepts are fine and good, but providing actual words we can use—That's pure parenting gold."
Teri Cettina, contributing editor, *Parenting* magazine

"A down-to-earth parenting book written by a real expert—one who has been in the trenches with her own children and taught parenting to others for 25 years. Full of wisdom and experience… for multiple situations real-life parents face."
Janet Gonzales-Mena, author of *Dragon Mom*, student of Magda Gerber

"We are all rookies, especially with that first child. Many of us have said things like "I was spanked and I turned out just fine." But if we really dig deep, is fearing your parents "just fine"? *Stop Reacting and Start Responding* helps parents respond so a child's decisions aren't tied to fear."
Tracy Harkins Ross

"Sharon's book provides a better way by teaching us how to respond more effectively while making your child feel acknowledged and loved. This book is designed for busy parents to use as a tool in their arsenal of parenting skills— tools that work! Sharon's manner is caring yet firm and her analysis of situations is always on target. Her help works, and kids respond!"
Heidi MacLaren, *A Smart Cookie but Sometimes a Clueless Parent,* West Linn, Oregon

"It was refreshing to be able to quickly reference tips and not have to read a book cover to cover in order to feel prepared to institute the strategies identified. After reading Sharon's book, I came away feeling refreshed and refocused on my vision of the kind of parent I want to be."
Rachel Fouts-Carrico, MEd, mother and teacher

"Sharon really does seem to see the entire relationship between parent and child in our interactions in a way that most authors and experts don't. I think my entire parenting experience would have been easier if I'd known about her work when my older one was younger."
Moxie, *AskMoxie.org*

Acknowledgments

Writing this book has been transformational, my deepest gratitude to those who mentored me through this process. Your support, wisdom, and advice helped me grow and prepared me to write this book.

To Mom and Dad, my love is a given. What I want to acknowledge and thank you for are the choices you made as I was growing up. They broadened my view, and in hindsight, were exactly what I needed.

To Mom, Dad and Benny, you gave me an extremely rare view of how three different people parented. Growing up with you sparked my interest in learning more about families and parenting. Thank you.

To my sister, my love and admiration are also a given. You're an amazing mother whose sweet son is a true testament to all that you and hubby are, strong, happy and joyful.

To my in-laws and extended in-law family. You welcomed me into your very large family years ago and lovingly let me see how a big family interacts and loves one another. I've learned so much.

To my children—you know I'm a mush ball when it comes to the two of you! I loved every moment of each of your childhoods, okay, not *every* moment. I'm honored to be your mother—I adore both of you!

To my husband, my love and partner in life. Thank you for being the gentle, powerful soul that you are, for always having my back, for having faith that this book would happen, and for always doing whatever it took to make it happen.

To Candace Lienhart, the ultimate instructor and friend. Thank you for your truth, wisdom, humor and willingness "To do the dance until I picked up the steps." Thanks to you and the "support team" for telling me the truth and helping me to see who I am, and for the fun!
www.kahunakindergarten.com

Thanks to T. Berry Brazelton for the highlight of my career, so far—the note you sent saying I was "indeed correct" after I had the audacity to correct *you*. That meant the world to me.

To Janet Gonzales-Mena for your warmth, encouragement, wisdom and for pushing me to honor my true calling. You saw something in me that, at the time, I didn't see in myself. I will always be grateful.

To Robyn Mather for showing up out of the blue because you didn't want anyone to steer me in the wrong direction. Your coaching support and ability to convert a website is magical. www.robynmather.com

To Suzanne Paquette for creating my logo. Thank you for translating who I am onto the page—a rare talent!
suzanne.sixdegrees@gmail.com

To Off Ramp Publishing, your family was right Lorraine; you were born with a red pen in your hand.
www.offramppublishing.com

To Judi Moss for your amazing editing. You see details like no one else I know. I couldn't have done this without you!
judi@anextrahand.com

To Michelle Radomski of One Voice Publishing, there are no words! You did so much more than design this book from cover to cover. You've been my guiding light, my rock when things went south, my cheerleader when things went well, and have become a dear friend! You're gifted and guided;

you took my vision and gave it wings to fly. Anyone would be lucky to have you as a designer and publisher!
www.OneVoiceCan.com

To the parents reading this. I hope you found, after implementing the tips in this book, that your children really did rise to your expectations as a result of being treated with respect, and taught, not punished for their lack of experience. Happy parenting!

Table of Contents

Chapter 14: Siblings

Chapter 15: Travel

How To Use This Book~A Must-Read

Let me start this book by being very clear. I'm not presumptuous enough to think for one moment that I have something completely new to share with you. What I do have to offer is a unique way of looking at parenting. At least that's what parents have told me for the last 25 years. My job, as I see it, is to help parents see the big picture as it relates to what's going on in the moment. Having that information allows parents to stop reacting and begin responding.

You, like any other parent, want to be the best parent you can be. All parents have times when parental reactions replace thinking. It's at that moment when you want to be reminded of how you've chosen to parent. It's at that moment when you need your restraint to kick-in. It's at that moment when you want to use discipline consciously so you can respond, not simply react and punish—again.

This book is for parents who have children ages one through ten. I focus on that age group because I firmly believe that ages one through ten are the foundational years of life, the time when parents are learning to parent, and children are just learning about life. What's created during those years tends to dictate how the rest of childhood and parenting will go. It's also the easiest time in life to change your parenting style, before reaction habits are set in stone for both parent and child.

Believe me when I tell you I'm not an advocate of strict or permissive parenting. I'm not at all interested in letting children off-the-hook. Quite the opposite in fact, ask my kids! I am an advocate of loving, supportive, empathetic, firm, clear, and unyielding parenting which respectfully teaches children about behavior and life. That's what I describe as disciplining consciously.

Correcting behavior and enforcing boundaries is the hardest work you'll do as a parent. It's your personal walk through fire for your child. It's that important to his or her development. Correcting behavior and setting boundaries are the true teachers and life lessons of childhood. And parents are the ones enforcing them, like it or not. The question is how to do it and can it be done with love? Yes, it can! This book shares new ways to discipline consciously, and do it without reacting, while still being firm enough to create change. In other words, the book shows you how to create a balance between the job of correcting a child and loving a child.

I believe that anything transformative is usually simple at its core. So I've written the tips in that style, as simply as possible, so there's no confusion. The tips are short and filled with many layers of information. Sometimes changes will occur instantly, and sometimes changes will unfold as you and your child gain more and more wisdom from applying the new techniques.

The book is divided into chapters and then into situations that parents encounter on a daily basis. A quick view is presented at the end of each tip so you can refer back to the method, get a thumbnail version, and then turn right around and use the technique.

I highly recommend that you begin with the first tip as it prepares you for the rest of the book.

The mistakes and typos in this book are my gift to you. I hope they'll remind you that there's no perfection in parenting or in life!

Please remember, this is my view of parenting. It's up to you to pick and choose what you think will work for you and your family.

Happy Parenting!

CHAPTER

1

BEHAVIOR

1. Battle of Wills ~ How It Begins

A battle of wills, normal as it is, is one of the hardest things a parent and child will deal with. Most parents believe that the battle is the child's fault. When I look at a battle of wills, I see two sides, each one valid, yet destined to collide with the other. Let me explain.

Suppose you find a tip you want to try. It resonates with you because it's gentle and firm at the same time. Halfway through using the new technique your child's behavior seems to be getting worse. You wonder what could be making her react, especially since the method is calmer and more peaceful than the yelling she's used to. You begin to wonder if the method is failing, and think about giving up.

The reason your child is reacting is because she wants the "old normal" to prevail. You know, the way it was yesterday and the day before, even though the old way involved yelling and punishing. To her, the old normal was familiar. The parent, on the other hand, is reaching for the "new normal," the way he or she wants things to be from now on. Those two opposing points of view collide, creating the battle of wills.

The reason your child feels so uncomfortable is because you're so calm. When parents yell, children tend to retreat emotionally in order to withstand the yelling. The yelling prevents your child from feeling how firm you really are because she's busy protecting herself from the intensity of it. When you remove the yelling, your firmness takes center stage, and that's powerful. Feeling your authority and the unmovable boundary causes her to feel unsettled and throw everything she has into a battle of wills hoping to make things return to what she perceives as normal.

After all of that, who wouldn't wonder if the method is failing? The truth is the method is not failing; parent and child are in the middle of the process. I call the middle of the process the *danger zone*. It's the place just before change occurs, the place when a parent wants to give up.

You have to push past the feeling of wanting to give up or you'll have to begin the method again at another time and endure the entire battle of wills all over again. You need to hang in there and remain calm so you can show your child that this is the way things are going to be from now on. If you lose your temper, or things get really out of hand, then stop, re-read the tip and begin again.

You can be supportive, too. Tell her you know she doesn't like the new rule, but this is the way it's going to be. Invite her to sit on your lap or give her a hug, if she'll allow you to. Doing that helps her feel safe enough to make the shift to the new way of doing things.

So the next time you find yourself knee deep in a battle of wills and you want to give up because you think the method has failed, know that you're in the *danger zone,* the middle of the process, and hang in there just a little while longer in order to create change.

Quick View

- Children create a battle of wills to try and get the "old normal" to return.
- Parents participate in the battle to push for the "new normal" to begin.
- This battle represents the middle of the process, the *danger zone.*
- Push past the feeling of wanting to give up to show a child that this is the way things will be from now on.

2. Lying ~ Punishing Isn't the Answer

We all know that children lie to try and get out of taking responsibility for something they've done. Lying is a normal, natural part of childhood. It falls under the heading of "experimenting."

Due to development, children believe if you can't see something, then it isn't really there. For example, if I cover my eyes, I can't see you. That also means you can't see me either. They experiment with lying to see if the same principal applies to lying too. They think if I make a mistake and lie, or hide the truth from you, you'll believe me because the truth is *hidden*. When you understand lying from a child's point of view you can see that it's better to deal with a lie by teaching than by punishing.

When a child fails to tell the truth, all parents become afraid they have a liar on their hands. The parent reacts making a big deal out of the lying, hoping to stop any lies from ever happening again.

Some parents accuse their child of lying so often that the child comes to believe he's a liar. Each time the child gets into a sticky or uncomfortable situation, his first response is to lie even though he's punished heavily for it.

Some parents do the exact opposite. These parents handle lying in a way that shows their child they have faith in his ability to tell the truth. Their support reduces some of the fear he has about owning up to the truth.

So, how can a parent handle lying with support instead of punishment? Parents can activate a lie-free/consequence-free-zone when they suspect a lie has been told. Have a meeting with your child and let him know you believe he's honest and sometimes says things that aren't true. Tell him if you suspect a lie has been told, you'll activate a 10-minute lie-free/consequence-free-zone so he can tell the truth. Here are two other ways to handle lying if you don't like the lie-free/consequence-free-zone.

Try treating "lying" as if it were a tall tale instead of lying. Your words will still convey the fact that you know he isn't telling the truth, and for most children, that's more than enough pressure to cause them to fess-up. Here's an example: "Wow, what a story! I know you, and you always tell me what happened. Why don't you try again?"

One last way to handle lying is to repeat the request and skip over the lie. Suppose you've asked your child to brush her teeth, and she claims that she did it, but you know she didn't. Instead of accusing her of lying, skip over the lie and repeat your request. Say, "I hear what you're saying, and I'm asking you to go and brush your teeth."

There's no need for further punishment with any of methods, unless the lie is very serious. By handling lying this way you've created a safe place for your child to do the necessary childhood experimenting without casting him into the role of a liar. Whichever way you choose to handle lying, remember that your words tell your child who you believe him or her to be, which helps shape the view he has of him or herself.

Quick View

- Have a family meeting and announce the 10-minute lie-free/consequence-free-zone.
- Try treating the lie as if it were a tall tale.
- You can also skip over a lie and simply repeat your original request.

3. New Attitude ~ It's Not Just a Song

I don't remember who said, "Falling apart is just falling together in a new way," but that's how I explain child development. When a child is going through a developmental phase, his world is turned upside-down. He can't sleep, or he sleeps a lot; he doesn't want to eat, or you can't give him enough food; he's clingy, or he wants nothing to do with you, and so on.

The developmental phase is advancing his way of looking at the world, causing him to have a different perspective, an older, more developed perspective. When the phase is complete, a child will seem like his old self again, only different.

Most likely his new view of the world will subconsciously cause him to re-test some of the old rules that you thought were firmly established. He isn't being bad; he just needs to see if those old rules apply to the "new me." When testing does occur, make sure to correct the behavior as you normally would. Don't skip over misbehavior because you know that it's the result of a developmental phase. Being consistent with rules and boundaries creates a sense of trust and safety he relies on as he integrates the new development.

Just knowing that re-testing is highly likely after a developmental phase can shift the way you feel about his misbehavior, and increases the odds that you will be able to respond, not react.

Quick View

- When your child's behavior is falling apart, it's probably a developmental phase.
- Once the phase is fully integrated you'll experience a familiar, yet seemingly new child.
- Re-testing of previously established rules is likely. Be consistent with rules to create a sense of safety and trust.

4. One More Chance ~ What a Child Hears

When you say, "I'm giving you one more chance," think about what you've just said.

Children don't understand the nuances in language until they are much older. When you say, "I'm giving you one more chance to listen to me!" a child doesn't see that as a warning to listen or else. A child hears, "I get one more chance; I get extra time to play!" That's age-appropriate concrete thinking.

Saying, "I'm giving you one more chance to hear me!" also tells your child that you don't really expect him to listen to you the first time around. One more chance can easily turn into two, and then three more chances, and may cause your child to think he doesn't need to listen to you at all.

To break that cycle, simply stop saying, "I'll give you one more chance to listen to me!" and follow through when he doesn't do as asked the first time. Your child will react when you do that. This is the moment when you hold firm and respond, not react. You respond by being supportive, as you hold the boundary firm. You can say, "I know this is hard and you don't like it, but I asked you once and I meant it." Lovingly holding the boundary firm is how things will change. Sooner, rather than later, he'll be listening the first time, because he knows there are no more chances.

Quick View

- Think about the words "I'm giving you one more chance!" from the child's point of view.
- A child hears, "I get some extra time to play."
- Hold firm to your request and follow-through to stop your child from doing something; don't give him "one more chance."

5. Repetition ~ Frustration for Two

Some days, when you're so frustrated with your child's behavior you think, "Will my child ever learn?" We've all been there; you're not alone.

Repetition is totally normal and necessary. It's how children learn—and it's frustrating. Children repeat things over and over again in order to learn every nuance of a rule, activity or situation. And each time they go through a developmental phase, they repeat things.

How many times did your child stand up and sit down before she learned to walk? How many times did she try to insert a square block into a round hole before she learned a round block goes in a round hole? How many tries did it take her to ride a bike, play basketball, or color inside of the lines? This type of learning was frustrating to her, but you didn't join her in her frustration. You stayed beside her and supported her with empathy and understanding. You reached out to help her learn when you thought she needed it, not when she became frustrated. You encouraged her because you knew she had to move through her frustration so she could figure out how to do it. Her growth was obvious because you could see it.

As children get older, their growth becomes less visible. They still need things to be repeated in order to learn, and you still need to be empathetic and understanding when you reach out to help them learn.

Teachers really understand how important repetition is. Think about how a teacher teaches the alphabet. Does she say, "This is the letter "A": memorize it because you will never see it again?" No, the children sing songs with the letter "A" in it. They read stories about the letter "A." They write words that contain the letter "A." They repeat and repeat using every possible method to learn about the letter "A."

So the next time you're frustrated and about to shout, "How many times have I told you?" remember, she's not really being disobedient. There's just some part of her that isn't finished learning about this situation or rule yet. You'll be surprised at how remembering this will shift you from feeling frustrated to willing to do some more teaching.

Quick View

- If your child exhibits frustration, don't join her frustration; be a source of support.
- It's okay to lovingly push a child through the frustration when beginning something new. That's how learning occurs.

6. Either/Or ~ Reminder-Choice

Tip #5 addressed frustration, both yours and your child's, and hopefully began reducing your reactions, too. A reduction in reactions means you're no longer forcing your child to jump over the hurdles of your anger and frustration as part of the learning process, and that creates a more direct pathway to the learning. This tip addresses the other part of the learning that needs to occur: the correction.

Parents want to know how to correct repeated misbehavior, how to do it without reacting, and how to be supportive so a child can learn at the same time. Yes, sometimes when a child needs to be corrected, a consequence does need to occur. There are also times when the learning can be more organic and simply be addressed with support and boundaries. This tip encompasses all of these needs and uses a correction, if need be.

This tip refers to a reminder-choice. A reminder-choice is a statement or choice a parent uses to *respond* to a situation without using long explanations or punishment. It reminds the child of the rules by restating a boundary or a rule, and tells your child what will happen if the rule isn't followed, and it's all neatly done in one sentence. The way the statement or choice is delivered is what creates a direct pathway to learning.

When creating a reminder-choice, you'll use the word *either* or the word *or* and deliver the statement or choice in a firm, non-frustrated voice. A reminder-choice sends the silent message, "You know the rules, so I'm simply going to remind you in a way that leaves no room for misunderstanding. And if you still can't behave, then I'll take action." Here's an example:

Instead of saying, "How many times have I told you not to toss the baseball in Grandma's house? Give me that and get to timeout!" try saying, "Baseball is played outside or the ball is mine," or "You can either play with your ball outside or the ball is mine!" The taking of the baseball *is* the consequence.

You may be wondering, if he knows the rules, why not just give him a consequence for being disobedient?

My explanation is a rehash of tip #5.

- When a child goes through a developmental cycle he comes out of it with a deeper understanding of the world around him. He unconsciously revisits rules he knows really well to see if the rules have changed, now that he has changed. He's actually deeply comforted by the fact that the rules are the same.

- Additionally, if you use consequences and punishment for everything during childhood, there's a good chance it will negatively impact the relationship you have with your child, and create a lot of rebellion during the teen years. A reminder-choice allows you to be consistent, accomplish cooperation in an instant, and does it all by responding to the needs of the situation, not reacting to the misbehavior, and who doesn't want that!

Quick View

- A reminder-choice skips any long explanations and reminds a child about his behavior without lecturing.
- A reminder-choice restates a boundary or a rule, using the word *either* or the word *or* and tells your child what will happen if the boundary or rule isn't followed.

7. Shyness ~ Doing It Anyway

Sometimes a parent thinks pushing a shy, reluctant child beyond her comfort zone will help her get over her shyness. Forcing a shy child to go beyond her comfort zone can actually backfire, causing her to feel a sense of panic that only makes things worse. If you look at shyness from the child's point of view, most of the time you'll see that the shy child would love it if she weren't shy and reluctant, but she has no idea how to deal with the feelings that shyness produces.

Let me be very clear here. I had a very shy child, so I know that shyness is not really something that can or needs to be solved. I never insisted that my child move beyond his comfort zone until he was prepared. What I did do was stop avoiding his discomfort. I slowly helped him work *with* his discomfort until he realized that he could take his discomfort with him and do it anyway. This is what I want to share here.

One way to help a shy, reluctant child is to participate in the activity *with* them, not *for* them, and not by *forcing* them. You don't actually do the activity with them; you ask them questions about where they would like you to be as they take the leap of faith and move out of their comfort zone.

- "Do you want me to stand beside you or behind you when you walk into piano lessons?"
- "Do you want me to hold your hand or put it on your shoulder, as you ask if she can come out to play?"
- "Do you need to see my face or should I hide so only you know I'm here when you ring the doorbell?"

Each question tells your child that she'll need to do this by herself, but *with* your support. As she's learning to be courageous, remind her of the times she's been successful. Handling shyness in this way sends her the silent message, "*I know you can do it.*" She'll draw from your faith in her until she's been successful, by herself, enough times to prove it to herself. She'll remember that she can move past her fear and shyness because she's done it before.

Supporting her, and not doing things for her, creates a pathway, a memory that lives deep inside of her and shows her how to summon up the courage she needs to enter a situation she has not encountered before. She will remember and rely on that knowledge for years to come.

Quick View

- Forcing a shy child to go beyond her comfort zone can actually backfire.
- The key to helping a shy child is to stop avoiding her discomfort and work *with* it instead.
- Questions send the message she'll need to do this by herself, but *with* your support.

8. Stopping Mean Words ~ Pull the Plug

When a child says something mean to a parent, most parents react immediately. The parent thinks that if they react quickly, it will stop their child from using more mean words. The problem with that is acting quickly makes the situation worse. The parent goes from thinking clearly to reacting, and actually might use mean words in response to the child's angry words. And, of course, that causes the child to react and use even more mean words and so on.

When teaching children about not using mean words, it is easier to teach the lesson by responding instead of reacting. You can achieve that by saying, "I'm going to wait two minutes before I say anything. Please do the same so we don't continue to hurt each other's feelings." At that point, many children will realize immediately what has really happened.

Two benefits can occur when you choose this course of action. You get to calm down and disengage from the feelings so you don't have another reaction, and for two minutes your child gets to live with the fact that something is going to happen because she used the mean words. Two minutes can seem like a lifetime when you know you've been out of line. For some children that amount of silence may be all that's needed to create cooperation when you begin talking again. The rest of the tips in this book will tell you what to do from here.

Quick View

- Parents think reacting quickly to mean words will stop a child from using more mean words.
- Calling for silence disengages both of you from the heightened emotional reactions.
- For some children, two minutes of silence is all that's needed to create cooperation.

$\mathcal{9}$. Waking Up ~ All by Myself

As you read this book, my hope is that you'll get the sense that your *true* job is to prepare your child for the world beyond your front door. Using an alarm clock to wake up is something we all eventually have to learn to do.

Since younger children love to do things *all by themselves,* why not capitalize on that fact when it comes to introducing an alarm clock? Set the alarm for five minutes *after* you want your child to get up. Go in and gently wake her up and then leave the room, allowing her to stay in bed. Tell her to wait until the alarm goes off before her feet hit the floor. Tell her she can even shut it off herself.

This gets her used to the jarring sound an alarm makes so when she's in elementary school she can manage this for herself. Doing this allows you to check another thing off the teaching-life-skills list.

$\mathcal{Q}$uick View _____

- Set the clock for five minutes *after* you want your child to wake-up.
- Gently wake her up as you always have.
- Tell her to wait until the alarm goes off before her feet hit the floor.
- Let her turn the alarm off by herself, and then check-in with you so you know she's up.

10. Yelling ~ Acting on a Misconception

Every parent has days when she feels as though all she's done is yell all day long, and it didn't change a thing. Those are the days when you feel defeated and want to run away. Before you pack your bags, let me share one possible reason why your yelling isn't working and suggest a way to change things.

Young children gravitate to where they experience the most energy. When a parent yells, he or she exudes a great deal of energy and, wait for it, attention.

Think about it, what do you do when you yell? You stop what you're doing, you turn around, you lock eyes with your child and you focus all of your words on him. That's a lot of attention! Children gobble that up, and then use child-like thinking and decide that misbehavior is a good way to get their parent's focused attention, even though they're yelling. I know it's hard to believe that children think they're getting attention when a parent yells, but that's immature thinking in action. Children don't see the whole picture yet, so they don't really know that behaving well is a better way to get Mom or Dad's full, undivided attention, unless you show them, repeatedly.

The best way to change your child's mind about how to get fully focused attention from you is to shift where *you* put the majority of *your* attention. Shift your focus, attention and words to what you want your child to be doing—rather than focusing on what he's done. That simple process will cause a huge increase in listening and cooperation, and reduce your yelling tremendously.

Spend a week making a bigger deal out of what he does right, rather than what he does wrong, and watch what happens! When you do have to correct him, make it clear, firm and short. The tips in this book will help you with that.

If there isn't much he's doing right that you can comment about, then concentrate on the little things until it gets better. Focus on things like how well he ate his cereal or how he didn't fight with his sister. This will show him that behaving well gives him all kinds of focused attention, like compliments, hugs, appreciation, or bragging about him to Dad or Grandma. It also shows him that when he misbehaves, you're calm and can now handle things more firmly and quickly.

He'll soon recognize what kinds of behavior get him "good" attention and begin to produce better behavior more consistently in order to get pleasant, non-yelling attention. This really does work. For another way to look at this solution, read tip #17.

Quick View

- Children use age appropriate thinking and decide that misbehavior is a good way to get a parent's focused attention, even if it means being yelling at.
- Spend a week focusing on what's being done *right*, rather than on what's being done *wrong*.
- Soon he'll see that "good" behavior gains him more attention than "bad" behavior and he'll produce better behavior.

CHAPTER

2

CHOICES

11. Choices ~ Threats Not Included

I hear a lot of parents offering what they perceive as a choice, except the choice they use has an implied threat woven into it. It sounds like, "Do you want to pick up the toys or get a timeout?" or "Turn that computer off now or go to your room, you choose!" The parent seems genuinely surprised when the child screams, "No!" When I ask a parent about the way he or she has framed the choice they say, "Well, I gave her a choice."

As a former Love and Logic instructor (the people who made choices popular), I know three important things parents need to understand about offering choices that will help them to enforce a choice without threatening or punishing. I'm going to paraphrase what Jim Fay, one of the founders of Love and Logic, says about choices:

1. Children can really only handle choosing between two choices. Offer a choice with two options only.
2. Make sure you approve of *both* choices. Choices only work when a child is free to choose either pre-approved option.
3. Structure the choice so it's clear that if the child doesn't choose, you will choose for her, or the choice will no longer be offered, whichever is appropriate for the situation.

Here are two sample conversations. The first one shows what it sounds like when the choice includes limitless possibilities. The second conversation shows what it sounds like when all that's offered are two parent-approved choices. Notice that the choice also makes it clear what will happen if the child doesn't choose.

Dad: "What do you want to drink?"
Child: "Coffee!"

Dad: "Come on, we're in a hurry! You know you can't have coffee! Choose again!"
Child: "A latte."
Dad (beginning to get mad and threatens): "Make the right choice or get nothing!"
Child: "Okay, I'll have a lemonade!"
Mom: "Wait a minute, that's too much sugar."

Here's the same conversation rephrased, in which the parent limits the choices to two parent-approved options.

Dad: "Would you like apple juice or milk?"
Child: "I want coffee."
Dad: "Nice try, I'm only offering juice or milk."
Child: "I want a latte!"
Dad: "You can choose juice, milk, or nothing. What do you want?"

I believe that offering choices is a powerful tool for children. I also know that if the choice isn't offered the way it's outlined, it can easily cause the power struggle you were hoping to avoid in the first place.

Quick View

- Offer children two 100% parent-approved choices only.
- Choices only work when a child feels totally free to choose the pre-approved choice *she* wants.
- Make sure to include information that tells your child that if they don't choose, you will choose for them.
- Writing about choices makes it impossible to explain the tone of voice parents need to use. Please note, that in the first example the parent is frustrated. His choice of words communicates this. In the second example the parent is firm and clear. That example works because the firm, clear words are delivered in a loving calm voice.

12. "Do It Now!" ~ Demand or Empower?

Now that you know the three things needed to empower your child to choose, how do you, the parent, make it clear that your child has to do as asked, *now*? The key is to give him some power in a world where his parents traditionally make all the decisions.

Any choice you create needs to be phrased in a way that tells your child that the task is going to get done *now;* there is no choice about that. To gain cooperation, allow her to have some power regarding how she does the task.

Example of a Demand

Mom: "Pick up your toys, now!"

That's a demand with no choice attached to it. Most likely your child will feel powerless, resist you and *react* or protest as she picks up the toys. Then you'll *react*, and the arguing and fighting begin.

The examples below will show you how to create a choice that can empower her cooperation, and how to *respond* if she chooses *not* to pick up the toys. Remember, as stated in tip #1, when you remove the yelling, your firmness takes center stage, and that's powerful. Also, notice that there are only two choices offered by the parent.

An Empowered Choice for a Younger Child

Mom: "You need to pick up the toys. Do you want me to sing the pick-up song or put on some other music while you pick up the toys?" or "Do you want to pick up the toys by color or just scoop up what goes in each basket?" or "Do you want to use a timer and try to beat yesterday's record or just do it by yourself? Please choose or I will choose for you."

An Empowered Choice for an Older Child

Mom: "Your five-minute alarm to get off the computer is ringing. Would you like to shut the game down now before another game begins, or are you willing to shut the computer off in the middle of the next game? Please decide now, or I will decide for you."

The choice makes it clear that a decision will be made now and shows what part of the decision he has a choice about; *when* to shut the computer off, and the part he doesn't have a choice about, the computer *is being* shut off. He's also clearly told what will happen if he doesn't make a choice.

Offering choices when a child is young helps make choices a part your family's vocabulary. Knowing that choices are the norm in your family will help you better deal with the power struggles in later years.

Quick View

- The key is to give a child some power in a world where parents traditionally make all the decisions.
- Any choice needs to be phrased so a child knows the task is to be done *now*; there are no choices about that.
- Cooperation is gained when your child is allowed to have some power regarding *how* she does a task.
- Remember, the fact that you're not yelling creates instant firmness. The tone of voice you use to deliver that firmness can absolutely be warm, kind and respectful.

13. Choosing Not to Choose ~ What to Do?

You read in Tip #12 that the parent asks her child to make a choice or she will make the choice for her. That's the place in the conversation when things begin to get a little bit more difficult.

When a child won't make a choice, he's not being bad; several things could be going on.

- He could be afraid to make a choice because making one choice means the other choice goes away. He's too young to understand, without your help, that choosing one thing simply means he can choose the other thing tomorrow.

- He could be in the throes of a developmental phase and unconsciously need to know what will happen when he doesn't make a choice.

- He's trying to find out who holds the power in the situation, you or him. He wants to know, "Does Dad mean what he says?"

It may seem harsh to follow-through by making a choice for your child and go through all that drama, but there's a bigger concept in play here. What you're really teaching your child is that he needs to listen to his parent, and that lesson just happens to be playing-out through a choice at that moment. Teaching a child to listen is easiest if it's done *before* the age of five, the age when the brain is hard-wired, but anytime before the age of ten works as well. You will definitely need your child to know you mean business before the tween years.

Here are three key points:

- You need to know that making a choice for your child *will* cause tears, anger or tantrums. Knowing ahead of time gives you a better chance of being able to stay calm in the face of all the emotions. That calmness isn't lost on your child. It's translated as firmness, showing him that you mean it when you say, "Please choose or I will choose for you."

- Express empathy when you have to make a choice for your child. Go ahead and tell him you understand that he doesn't like it, you love him, and you're not changing your mind.

- Don't pile on more consequences because your child is upset. The fact that you made the choice for him is difficult enough. If you add more punishment, resentment or anger will take hold and the learning stops. Adding empathy, however, forces the lesson to take center stage. If the upset persists, you can always tell him to take his crying into his room, where he can cry all he wants, and he can come get a hug as soon as he's finished.

You need to be strong once you begin, otherwise the learning shifts away from choices and proves that, if he cries long and hard enough, you'll give in. I hear parents say all the time, "How can I make my child listen to me?" This is how you do it, and it's not always pretty.

Quick View

- There *will* be tears when you choose for your child. Stay calm and allow your firmness to take center stage.
- Express love and empathy. Tell him you know he doesn't like this and you're not changing your mind.
- Don't add more consequences because of the upset, or the learning stops.

14. When the Negotiations Begin ~ Oh, No

One day your child may push the boundaries you've set by asking, "Can we use my choice instead?" You'll probably be attracted to the idea of letting her. However, you may want to rethink that decision after reading this tip.

If you allow your child to use her choice instead of yours, she'll most likely interpret that to mean she's now allowed to insert her choice into the mix whenever a choice needs to be made. And constant negotiations will have begun.

This is another situation where listening to a parent is at stake. She isn't doing this because she's bad or willful; she's simply entered the phase of learning about negotiating and trying to figure out if she has the power to change your mind. I won't lie here; it is easier to let her add her choice, but doing that changes the situation into a more complex issue. The power she gains may cause her to test your authority in other ways, too. To spare yourself the misery of constant negotiations, you'll need to make it clear who's in charge of offering choices and presenting options.

The following is an example showing a child that Mom and Dad are the only ones who offer choices.

Mom: "That's a pretty good choice you just shared, but today you need to choose from the two choices I offered."

Child: "But why? I want to use my choice; I want the apple, not the veggies!"
Mom: "Because parents are the makers of the choices, not children, and that's the rule. But I'll remember your creative choice for next time, and *maybe* we can use it then!"

If things move into a power struggle or a tantrum, go to the table of contents, and find the situation you're dealing with. The tip will help you deal with these challenges as well.

Quick View

- Negotiating and testing boundaries is normal and is evidence that your child has entered a new developmental phase.
- To stop constant negotiations, make it clear who's in charge of offering choices.
- There's a good chance experimentation with negotiations will show-up in other situations too.
- The most important thing to remember, in order to be successful, when you offer a choice is the tone of voice you use. Make sure to deliver your choice in a loving and empathetic way so the child can't protest the way you framed the choice.

15. Lightening the Mood ~ Silly Works, Too

Who said parents should only offer choices in a serious, I'm making-a-boundary type of voice? You can really lighten the mood by playing with choices.

One of my favorites is, "The chef is offering cereal or yogurt this morning. Which one would you like, your majesty?" Children think it's funny and are so willing to choose when it's fun and light.

Try saving your firm, I'm making-a-boundary type of voice for the times when you really need it. Waiting to use your firm voice creates a better chance that they'll listen and adhere to the boundary because the firm voice is so different, and less often used, than your everyday, light-hearted, fun voice.

Quick View

- "Silly" is a great way to get a child to cooperate and make choices.
- Some children are serious children when it comes to rules. You know your child best, and know whether or not being silly will cause more trouble than it's worth.
- If you can save your firm, I'm making-a-boundary voice for the times when you really need it, there's a better chance your child will really listen, because the firm voice is such a contrast to the silly voice.

CHAPTER

3

FEELINGS

16. Apologies ~ Don't Be Rude!

A time will come—maybe it's happened already—when your child will say something in a way that's rude or filled with an attitude. You'll address the situation, and of course, require her to say, "I'm sorry." Most children will say it respectfully and mean it. There are times, however, when a child's "I'm sorry" can stop sounding genuine and sound more like a sassy "sooorrreee." When a child uses a sassy "I'm sooor-rreee," it's the perfect moment to begin teaching her that her words have power, and that the way her words are delivered can prevent them from sounding genuine.

One way to teach that message is to change your response from, "That was rude; say 'I'm sorry' right now," to using a physical description that lets her know what those words felt like to you. For a younger child, you might say, "Ouch, that hurt my heart," or "Screaming mean words at me really hurts my ears and upsets my heart." For an older child, you could say, "Those words felt like arrows were attached to them" or "I felt anger in those words."

By clearly stating how those words impacted *you* emotionally, your child can begin to see the damage words can do. Responding this way teaches a far more powerful lesson than simply insisting she say, "I'm sorry." When a child is raised knowing the damage words can do, she may be less tolerant of bullying or cruelty to others.

Be aware that if you use words like this to inform your child of what her words did to *you*, a time may come, when yelling at *her*, you may hear "Ouch, that hurt my heart" being said back to you.

I think that's okay. Hearing that may remind you that you're the biggest role model your child has, and allows you the opportunity to show her how to rephrase statements so they are less hurtful. You'll have to decide if you agree that what's good for the goose, is good for the gander.

Quick View

- When "I'm sorry" stops sounding genuine, let your child know what those words feel like to you.
- When you make a child responsible for what comes out of her mouth, she may be less likely to tolerate bullying or being unkind to others.

17. Attention ~ Yelling Can Be Yummy

All parents have been told, "Ignore her: all she wants is attention." The problem with that is the way a child translates that advice. Because she doesn't have much life experience and uses immature thinking, she interprets being ignored to mean, "I better make my needs louder and bigger so maybe you *will* pay attention to me." The parent sees increased misbehavior as disrespectful, manipulative, bad, call it whatever you like. The parent stops ignoring the child, reacts, and begins to yell and punish. Sound familiar?

Another problem with ignoring a cry for attention is the misunderstanding on which a child begins to base his life decisions. It may not cause a huge impact now, but it will most definitely cause big problems as the child gets a little older. Candace Lienhart, a very wise woman in my life, once shared this analogy with me; maybe it will help you understand how a child sees this situation.

Suppose the amount of attention and emotional energy you give a child feels like a fabulous snack that the child loves and craves. To a child, the positive attention is like getting a slice of parent pie. The problem is that, due to immature reasoning, a child also perceives getting negative attention as a slice of parent pie, too; it's just a smaller slice.

If the majority of your daily communication is expressed through statements such as "Stop it," "Don't you dare," or "That's not appropriate," then your child's day is filled with negative attention and reaction statements. She decides, based on her experience, that "I get Mom's full attention when I do something wrong." This, then supports her assumption that acting inappropriately will get your attention.

Why would she think that way? Think about what you do when you correct her behavior. You stop what you're doing, turn around, look her directly in the eyes, and speak only to her. Since focused attention is what she gets from misbehavior, she associates creating misbehavior as the way to get Mom's attention. Can you see why ignoring her only perpetuates the situation?

To change that, all you need to do is spend about a week or two catching her doing things correctly and make a much bigger deal out of that behavior than the misbehavior. Her perception regarding how she gets attention, i.e. "the parent pie," begins to shift and behavior changes.

Knowing and changing this is so worth doing *now*. Nobody wants a tween or a teen to rebel and act out in order to get a parent's attention!

Quick View

- When a child thinks he's being ignored, his behavior goes up a notch to force a parent to pay attention to him.
- If the majority of your daily communication is expressed through reactions, a child decides, "I get more attention when I misbehave than when I behave."
- To solve this problem spend a week catching your child doing things correctly and make a big deal out of it.

18. Birthdays ~ Teaching Gratefulness

Birthday parties are wonderful. They can also bring out the I-want-more-stuff side of a child. We've all seen a child grab a wrapped gift, rip it open, then throw it down two seconds later. Most parents see that and are appalled that their child could act that way.

We all dream that our child will have perfect manners as they open their gifts. They will savor the unwrapping of the gift, and tenderly open it and shout in surprise at what's inside, then run to the gift giver and give them a huge hug and "thank you" before moving on to the next gift. That's a more grown-up or highly refined behavior. Ripping a gift open is a normal, natural thing most children do.

Is it possible to teach a child to appreciate the gift giving as much as the gift itself? I believe it is. You do that by focusing on non-material things, in addition to the gifts, so he experiences what to really appreciate. Here are a couple of ideas so you can give your child what he truly yearns for: quality time with you!

A birthday wheel is a great way to make a birthday unique and personal. Decorate a paper plate or poster board by dividing it into as many options as you want to offer your child. Add a spinning arrow so your child can spin the birthday wheel of choices.

Here are some ideas for the slots of *The Birthday Wheel of Personal Attention.*

- One slot could be a private date with each parent. A date can range from 30 minutes to several hours. It's not the activity that matters; the one-on-one adventure is the real present. The child gets to choose what he or she wants to do on that date. It can be a lunch date, a picnic, a trip to a museum or an extra half hour at the park. Make sure to list the parent-approved date with Mom or Dad choices on the plate too, so the child can only choose what you've already agreed to.

- One slot on the wheel could be a "get-out-of-doing-this-today" pass. It could be a free pass from doing chores that day. It could be a pass excusing him from eating veggies, or from sharing with little brother, or to stay up for an extra half hour.
- The wheel could also have slots on it for choosing a special birthday meal. In the movie *The Divine Secrets of the Ya-Ya Sisterhood*, the mother woke the birthday child up by sharing a tiny cake together before breakfast.

These ideas show a child where the real gift is; it's spending time with those he loves, and getting gifts!

Quick View

- Appreciation of gifts, and appreciation of the amount of time and energy you spend on a party, is something that's taught to a child over time.
- Be aware that elaborate birthday parties may require you to top last year's party.
- A birthday wheel usually causes a child to overflow with gratitude, because the gifts are things you're doing together, versus gifts she plays with alone.

19. Bossiness ~ Important for the Future?

Most parents become embarrassed when their child is being bossy. They cringe when they see their child attempting to control a situation, or telling others how to play the game the "right" way. There is another way to look at bossiness. Bossiness is a child's attempt to practice her developing leadership skills, but since she's young, she does it in an unrefined way. If you can look at her bossiness that way, you may become more inspired to teach her how to be a good leader instead of punishing her for being bossy.

A child needs to know that forcing friends to do things her way can scare them, make them angry, or stop them from wanting to play with her. If she phrases it nicely, however, she can tell a friend that she knows how to play the game the way the rules say, and she would be happy to show him, *if he wants*. That way the playmate gets to choose for himself if he wants that information. She also needs to know there's a very real possibility that her friend won't want to be shown anything. Children also need to know it's okay if someone doesn't want to play by the "exact" rules. There's always the option to play with something else, play beside each other doing different things, or choose another playmate.

She'll need to learn how to tell playmates things like directions and rules in a way that's kind and supportive, instead of mean, demanding and bossy. One great way to teach her the words to use, and when to say them, is to have her practice. Practicing with a young child really means acting things out through play. If you announce that you need to teach her something, she'll probably be less cooperative and hide her bossiness. But if you just play with her, and play with things in a way she perceives as *incorrect*, the stress will trigger her bossiness giving you the opportunity to do some teaching.

Offer her several examples, to help her figure out what to say or do to manage the situation in a less bossy way, and have her choose one to try. If she continues to be bossy, then do as a child would do, and simply ignore her. If she responds nicely, respect that she was able to do that, and stop talking or playing the way she's objecting to. Then switch roles and let her experience what it feels like to be the friend who is being bossed around. Role-playing is an excellent way to teach young children anything; it allows them to be themselves without the fear of punishment.

Remember, it's not about whether a child plays by the rules or not; it's about how the message is delivered.

Quick View

- Children accused of being bossy can turn out to be natural leaders if taught how to manage how they speak to others.
- Role-play is a great way to teach a bossy child how it feels to be the kid being bossed around, and how to express herself in a less bossy way.
- Teach a child that it's not about playing by the rules, or not, it's about how the message is delivered.

20. Bossy & The Screamer ~ Aha for Two

Constantly listening to the kids screaming, "Stop it!" or "I'm telling" at full volume is a challenge for any parent. The conversation between the siblings can become so loud and nasty that parents can lose their ability to think. Not being able to think limits a parent's ability to figure out how to get things back under control without reacting. Most parents will resort to punishing both children, hoping a timeout will finally stop things, but it seldom does, and 30 minutes later they're at it again. That's because there's only been punishment, no teaching or resolution.

It is obvious both children need to be taught a better way to manage the situation. Using discipline, instead of punishment, will empower them to better handle stressful situations by themselves. Teaching anybody only works when you don't make them feel "wrong" in the process. A great way to do that is to create opportunities for your children to have their own "aha" moment by asking a few questions instead of going directly to punishment.

Here's a sample conversation that zeros in on what each child needs to learn while the parent remains neutral.

Mom (addressing the bossy child) "When you were Sissy's age, was there a big sister to boss you around and tell you when you were wrong?"
Child: "No. But I *am* right 'cause I'm older!"
Mom: "You do know what's right, and that's good, but you learned it all by yourself, didn't you?"
Child: "Yes."
Mom: "Whose job is it to talk to children when they do something wrong?"
Child: "Only Mommy or Daddy."

Mom: "That's right. Don't you think Sissy should have the same chance to learn about right and wrong all by herself too?"
Child: "Yes."
Mom: "So instead of telling Sissy when she's wrong, tell me or Daddy and we'll take care of it."
Child: "Okay."

Mom (addressing the one being bossed): "When your sister says, "You're wrong" you get mad and scream, right?"
Child: "Yes."
Mom: "Would you like a chance to learn about right and wrong all by yourself?"
Child: "Yes!"
Mom: "Then maybe you should tell her that it makes you mad, instead of screaming at her?"
Child: "But she still tells me I'm wrong!"
Mom: "Well, we talked to her and she's willing to let you learn by yourself *if* you stop screaming at her. Would that work?"
Child: "Yes!"

Explaining things this way allows both children to be heard, it individually addresses the areas where they need to learn, and it's all done without really making anyone wrong.

Quick View

- To help the bossy child and the screamer, use discipline, which is teaching, instead of punishment.
- Using discipline allows you to remain neutral enough to ask questions and focus on each individual child's learning needs, while still giving them the opportunity for their own "aha" moment.

21. Discipline Consciously ~ S.T.R.R.

There *will* be times when a parent needs to convey that this is the end of the line. It's how you convey that message that determines whether learning or resentment, and possible future rebellion occurs. Reacting and sending a child to timeout is how most parents handle things, but it's not always the most effective route to take.

Suppose your six-year-old took a bag of potato chips and went outside, again. He left a trail of chips that you're now stepping on across the kitchen floor, on the carpet in the family room, and across the deck.

Old way:

Dad: "Don't you ever listen? Get to timeout, NOW!"

Disciplining consciously has a child *stop* what he's doing, *think* about what he's done, *realize* what he should have done instead, and *resolve* the situation. The acronym S.T.R.R. represents **S**top. **T**hink. **R**ealize. **R**esolve. It will help you remember the concept.

New way:

Dad: "What a mess!" (The parent is mad, and rightfully so. What makes this a conscious discipline response and not a *reaction* is what comes next.)
Dad: "You need to *stop* what you're doing—do not take another bite." This is the *Stop* step.
"What do you think is wrong here?" This is the *Thinking* step.
"What should you have done instead?" This is the *Realize*-what-I've-done step.
"How will you clean this up?" This is the *Resolve* step.
Of course you'll ask those questions one at a time, allowing the child to answer in between.

Here's why S.T.R.R. works.

- When Dad says, "You need to stop what you're doing." he isn't reacting, yelling and sending him to timeout. He's responding and taking command of the situation asking his son to simply *Stop.* Dad's firm demeanor tells his son that he's been caught and needs to stand still and wait.
- All parents know it's too hard to yell and think at the same time. Since Dad's not reacting, he can *Think.* He's able to create a question that causes his child to think too. He asks, "What do *you Think* is wrong here?" Those words transfer responsibility for figuring out what's wrong to the child, and that creates real learning.
- When Dad says, "What should you have done instead?" and is silent as he waits for an answer, he's having his son *Realize* what rule(s) he broke. Here, again, the thinking stops a power struggle and an argument from being created.
- When Dad says, "How will you clean this up?" teaching is taking place. Dad waits patiently as his son figures out what he *should* have done and how he'll *Resolve* or fix the situation.

Using the acronym S.T.R.R. will help you remember how to stop reacting and start responding and be the parent you want to be.

Quick View

- Try using the acronym S.T.R.R. to remind children of what to do. **Stop. Think. Realize. Resolve.**
- Using this method will help keep both the parent's and child's emotions in check.

22. Control ~ A Yoga Ball Lesson

This tip deals with the control needed to manage unexpressed feelings, both negative and positive, versus releasing feelings as they arise. You'll need your imagination for this one. We've all seen the large yoga balls that people sit on. Imagine that you put one of those yoga balls into a swimming pool.

Think of what happens when you push down hard on a yoga ball and try to keep it still in the water. Not only will you have to use a great deal of pressure to keep the ball steady, but if there's any movement in the water, the ball will most likely skirt out from under you because of the pressure you're using to try to control it.

However, if you place one finger lightly on the yoga ball, and there's movement in the water, you can easily remain in contact with the ball, making it much easier to control.

The yoga ball in this analogy represents your feelings, and the water represents life. The yoga ball shows you that it takes a lot of energy, control and pressure to stuff your feelings, and much less energy to deal with and release your feelings when issues come up.

Unexpressed feelings can easily cause you to become overwhelmed and overreact when your child misbehaves or life throws you a curve ball. But if you release feelings as they surface, you'll find you can remain calmer. That's because you don't have a backlog of feelings that come pouring out all at once, which is one thing that can cause a forceful reaction.

Why do I bring this up? Because I know all parents want their children to have an easier time in life than they had. I believe that once you experience the difference between keeping your feelings all tucked away, and releasing them when they surface, you may want to rethink how you address the expression of feelings with your child.

If you're a parent who says, "Stop crying right now!" or "Suck it up and stop being a baby!" or "Babies cry, big girls don't!" you need to be aware that those are the comments that teach a child to stuff, swallow, hold onto or ignore feelings.

If you use the methods in this book to release your feelings, you'll be modeling how to do it in front of your child. She'll grow up with a habit of releasing feelings that will last a lifetime.

Quick View

- All unexpressed feelings, negative and positive, can easily cause you to become overwhelmed and possibly react.
- You'll find you can remain calmer, if you release your feelings when they surface.
- Changing how you address your feelings models, for your child, *how* to do it and gives her a better chance at growing up knowing how to release her feelings too.

23. Hospitals ~ Truth, Trust, Courage

A child's hospital experience is filled with many things—lack of power, a shortage of choices, pain, fear, strange people and strange experiences. Because this is a new situation, your child will be looking at how you react in order to gain the answers to the unasked questions she has. She will look at your face to determine how bad things are, reading your masked emotions and your body language.

All parents put on a happy smile and try to be brave for their child, but how far should you go? I think the better way to handle things is to tell the truth in an age-appropriate way without overwhelming your child. If you smile and tell her "This won't hurt," and then it does hurt, your child will have evidence that you lied and begin to wonder what else you're lying about. You will have lost some credibility at a time when you need it the most.

I'm not saying you shouldn't try to keep your child's spirits up while in the hospital. She needs to smile to heal. What I am saying is try to empower your child within the boundaries of the situation. How do you do that? Tell your child the age-appropriate truth, accompanied by a choice.

Make sure to sound loving and empathetic as you offer these choices or it may upset her even further. Here's an example:

Mom: "Sweetie, in a few minutes you have to have more blood drawn. I know you don't want to, but there are no choices about that. Yes, the needle will feel like a pinch, but we need to get you well. You do have six other choices though.

1. You get to decide if you want to take one, two, or three deep breaths before the nurse begins.
2. You get to tell the nurse when to begin. Do you want her to start on number three or number five?

3. You get to decide if you want to cry or not cry. Either way is fine with me.
4. You get to decide if you want to squeeze my hand or squeeze the sheet.
5. You get to decide if you want to keep your eyes open or closed while the nurse draws the blood.
6. And you get to decide which flavor of ice cream you want when it's all over. Why don't we practice the deep breaths now while we wait?" (This keeps her calm until the nurse arrives.)

Depending on the age of the child, you can also be truthful about the body, the medicine and how it heals. You can tell a child that the medicine that's being swallowed is going down the throat into the tummy and traveling like a railroad train to where the sickness is. Doctors and nurses recommend that adults envision what's going on in the body and send white light to the problem to heal it. Why not let a child use his or her imagination to do the same? After all, no one is better at using his or her imagination than a child.

Telling the truth and giving many choices allows a child to trust you enough to summon up *her* courage to better deal with the situation. Once courageous, she's more likely to be empowered enough to do whatever is needed to get well.

$\mathcal{Q}$uick View

- Children look to you, your body language, and emotions to find out what the truth is in any situation.
- Try to empower your child, within the bounds of the situation, by offering many choices.
- Be as honest as you can be so your child will trust you and know he can rely on your help to heal.

24. I'm Mad ~ A Way to Release It

One day, when my son was little, he came into the kitchen and said, "I need to get the mad out!" I snickered, thinking it was a joke, until I looked at him. Standing there with his hands on his waist, he was breathing like a bull about to charge, and looking at me for answers. I realized I had to think fast; he was serious and had no idea how to release his pint-sized tension.

When a child gets angry, his or her whole body feels that agitation. If they're unable to calm down, telling them repeatedly to "calm down" just won't do the trick. They need to do something that gives them a really clear understanding of the difference between mad and calm inside of their bodies.

Here's a list of physical activities a child can do:

- Jumping Jacks
- Run full speed up a hill
- Run in circles on your driveway or in your garage
- Play basketball
- Pound a piece of wood
- Pound real modeling clay (*It's very hard and requires a lot of strength to work it.*)
- Scream in a pillow
- Hit a pillow
- Begin digging a hole for a plant
- Sweep out the garage with a small broom

These kinds of activities release the pent-up frustration, cause heavy breathing, and create instant calming so the child can successfully "get the mad out."

Quick View

- Adrenaline is released when someone gets angry or "feels really mad."
- It's hard to calm down quickly after adrenaline has been released.
- Participating in a positive physical activity that causes heavy breathing can counteract adrenaline and calm someone down.

25. Insincere Apologies ~ A "Real Sorry"

We've all seen it happen. A child does something to upset or hurt someone and is told to go and say, "I'm sorry." The child, using an indifferent tone of voice says, "I'm sorry," then trots off to play. The person who has been hurt, and the parent, are left feeling as though the apology wasn't enough to repair the damage done, but don't know what else to do.

If apologies in your house seem to have an indifferent or sarcastic tone to them, maybe it's time to begin teaching your child another way to apologize so he understands how important apologies are and how important it really is to repair the emotional damage he has caused. This tip explores a new way to apologize that requires a physical act of kindness in order to say, "I'm sorry."

I learned this technique from *Redirecting Children's Behavior* when I taught their program many years ago. It's called a "Make-Up." Here's what you do:

- You'll need a recipe box and a few recipe cards.
- Put each family member's name and picture on a divider card and place several recipe cards in each person's section.
- Call a family meeting.
- During the meeting, write down what each family member decides would be an act of kindness that would make them feel better when someone has hurt his or her feelings. It can be a hug, a kiss, a drawing, taking out the trash, a shoulder massage, emptying the dishwasher, folding the laundry, raking the leaves, cleaning up the toys one evening, or vacuuming a room. It can be whatever the person wants, as long as it's age-appropriate and safe for children.
- Write one wish per card, some for small offenses and some for large offenses. Do about ten per person.

- Make sure to draw a picture depicting the "make-up" on each card so the younger children can see what has to be done too.
- Remember to create a "make-up" in case someone is mean to the dog or cat.

When a family member does something that requires an apology, that person should go to the "make-up box" and look under the person's name and picture for something they can do to "make it better." The person who committed the offense chooses what to do to "make up" for the offense he committed. This can really teach a child about different valid ways of saying "I'm sorry," especially when parents participate as well.

Since "make-ups" require physically doing something for someone else, a child learns how much time and energy it takes to repair the damage he's caused, which tends to cause him to think before acting the next time.

Quick View

- A "make-up" is a physical act of kindness that teaches a child what it takes to truly repair hurt feelings.
- Record on cards what family members want to make them feel better, if their feelings have been hurt.
- The person who committed the offense is the one who chooses what to do to "make-up" for the offense he created.

26. Deep Breathing ~ Use Pretend Candles

Children are natural deep breathers. Look at them closely; you'll see their chest and belly rise and fall effortlessly with each breath. When they're upset, however, the breath moves into the chest and becomes shallower.

An upset child can feel as if she's hyperventilating. She may even think her breath is behaving that way all by itself, and that's scary. As adults, we know that regulating your breathing calms you down. A child has no idea about this. So just telling her to "calm down" will most likely have no real effect on her. Giving her an image to focus on, when she's too upset to think for herself, shows her exactly what to do.

A great way to get a child to calm down and regulate her breathing is to have her blow out pretend birthday candles. Have you ever watched a child blow out candles on a cake? He or she seems to suck up all the oxygen in the room and then exhale until there's almost no breath left inside of them. The deep inhale activates deep belly breathing, and will almost instantly begin calming her down.

Blowing out pretend candles not only shows her *how* to breathe, it creates a memory that's a wonderful piece of self-knowledge which can be applied anywhere, at any time, and at any age.

Quick View

- Teach a child how to blow out pretend birthday candles when they're calm.
- When your child gets upset, have her take a deep inhale and then pretend to blow out a whole cake filled with candles.
- This breathing changes the focus from crying to blowing out candles, helping the child go from upset to calm.

27. Tantrums ~ Handling Each Type

We've all seen phony, bossy or demanding tantrums. Not *all* tantrums have manipulation at their core; some are caused by overloaded emotions. A frustrated or overloaded tantrum is telling you, "I've reached my limit. I can't handle any more." It's the emotionally overloaded tantrum that I'm speaking of here. And two-year olds aren't the only ones who have tantrums. Older children and adults have them too. We've all seen adults who are emotionally overloaded and act demanding, rude, insistent, and entitled.

I believe when an emotionally overloaded tantrum begins a parent *shouldn't* walk away, try to ignore it, send a child to his or her room or yell, "Stop it now." The child can't "stop it" as easily as you think, especially a very young child.

When a child has a tantrum due to being angry, frustrated, sad or mad, each sob brings on more and more intense feelings, until he feels flooded with emotion. He isn't trying to manipulate you—he's overwhelmed. He may hear his heart pounding loudly. He's taking very short breaths and doesn't know *how* to calm down. Imagine, at the exact moment when you feel totally out of control, the person you trust most in the world turns around and walks away. I think that just adds fuel to the fire.

What if, instead of walking away, you stayed close, making sure to be just far enough away to avoid getting hit or kicked? What if, instead of trying to talk him out of the tantrum, you quietly and lovingly said, "I know, I know," while he cried. The sound of your voice becomes an emotional anchor for him. He can't *really* distinguish what you're saying; he just feels better hearing the *sound* of your voice. When he's calmer, you can talk. Some children hate it if a parent says anything when they're crying, and some even want you to go away. With those children, be silent, or walk away, but stay close. Do what's right for your child. You know him best.

As soon as you see any calming happening, slowly begin to speak until he's fully calm. For little ones use a calm tone of voice and repeat over and over again, "I'm right here, I'm right here." For older children you can say, "Come get a hug when you're ready and then we'll talk."

The teaching needs to occur after he is calm. You need to help him learn what he can do to help himself when he's out of control. He needs to learn how to speak about his emotions in a way that can help him release them, not keep them stored up inside until they boil over. He also needs to learn how to take deep breaths so he can physically calm down as well.

And there's something you, the parent, needs to remember. Your child may be able to manage himself when he's calm, but when he's upset and overwhelmed, his skill set changes. He doesn't have access to as many skills when he's out of control as he does when he's in control. Think about what adults say after they've acted out: "I never would have acted that way unless I was really upset." The same thing applies to children.

Oh, and, by the way, when it comes to phony, bossy or demanding tantrums, I usually say, "Nice try!" and *do* walk away!

Quick View

- Some tantrums are born out of manipulation, and some are the result of being emotionally overwhelmed.
- Using a soft voice, instead of yelling, lets a child anchor himself to you until he calms down.
- Children don't have access to as many skills when they're out of control as they do when they're in control.

28. "It's Too Hard!" ~ Tell It Like It Is

It's always better to have faith in your child than to not have faith. I know that seems obvious, and it is, unless you're in the middle of reacting to behavior. When reacting, you, just like a child, are overrun with emotions that can cause you to say things you don't mean. Depending on what you say, your child could end up feeling as if you have no faith in her.

When a child is whining, complaining and saying, "This is hard for me" or "I can't do it," most parents aren't really listening to the words being said. They only hear the whining and want it to stop. Whining *is* irritating and can stop parents from responding. It can even cause them to blurt things out like, "Stop whining. It isn't too hard; you're just being a baby." The child hears that and focuses on the "You're just being a baby" part and reacts. She may begin crying, which causes yet another parental reaction, and so on.

In order to get the child to move past the whining, try telling it like it is. When things are hard, go ahead and tell her. "I know this is hard, and I know you don't want to do it, but I believe in you; I know you can do it." By telling it like it is, a parent is more able to tolerate the whining and refocus on the situation.

I'm not advocating you treat her like a grown-up and force her to deal with the harsh realities of life. After all, she is a child. Telling it like it is teaches her to keep going and not suffer over whatever it takes to get it done, and all children need to learn that.

Quick View

- Telling it like it is helps parent's prepare a child for the adult world, shows support and softens life's blow just a little bit.

29. Tone of Voice ~ Think Mary Poppins

Most parents, at one time or another, have asked their children if their ears were open or closed, or said, "Did you hear me? Have you ever considered that perhaps *your* tone of voice may be closing your child's ears to hearing you and stopping him from listening and cooperating?

We all know that a parent's words are his or her authority, and the tone of voice you use is the delivery system for that authority. Next time you use a harsh tone of voice to communicate something to your child, look at his face, notice his body language. Does it seem open and receptive to you? If not, you might want to consider changing your delivery system next time to help ensure your message has been heard. Remember a "spoon full of sugar helps the medicine go down."

Quick View

- Using a harsh tone of voice may actually stop a child from hearing and cooperating with a parent.
- Look at your child's face and body language when you use a harsh tone of voice. Does it seem open and receptive to you, or closed and non-responsive?
- Remember "A spoon full of sugar...."

$30.$ What's Wrong? ~ Nothing!

As adults, we all know that emotions are difficult to express when you're in the middle of feeling them. It's no different for children. In fact, depending on how young a child is, that child may view feelings as separate from herself, as things that live inside of her that she can't control.

When a child views feelings this way, it can be difficult for her to answer the question, "What's wrong?" and really express what she's feeling. There is a way to help a child access her feelings without putting her on the spot. You change the words *you* use.

When you see something is obviously wrong, instead of asking, "What's wrong?" change the words to, "I see a sad face. What does your sad face want to say right now?" Or, "I see a scared face. What does your scared face want to say?" Or, "I see an angry face. What does your angry face want to tell me?"

Having a "scared face" talk, allows a child to talk about what is scaring her. And that will help her feel less threatened and more in control of her fear.

Quick View

- Emotions are difficult to express when you're in the middle of feeling them.
- Children can view feelings as things that live inside of them that they can't control.
- Instead of asking, "What's wrong?" try stating the obvious by asking, "What does your sad face want to say?"

31. Whining ~ Does She Feel Heard?

We all know whining can be caused by many things. Most parents say, "Stop whining" or "Use your words," hoping the whining will stop immediately, but it rarely does.

Don't get me wrong, whining is irritating and does need to stop. You know your child can make requests without whining. She does it all day long. So the real question is what's going on with her at this moment that's causing her to make a whiney request? Yes, it could be hunger or lack of sleep, but it could also be her feeling jealous, excluded, fearful, or incapable. It could be an unexpressed need for some extra love or a million other things.

The whining could also be a way of expressing the feeling that your child doesn't feel heard. You may feel as if you hear her, but she may not *feel heard*. These are two different things. If a parent doesn't notice that his child doesn't *feel* heard, the next step the child unconsciously goes for is whining. When the whining is shut down, instead of exploring what's causing it, the a child will fight, begin a power struggle, or throw a tantrum to express the frustration she's feeling. Those feelings are going to come out somehow.

Think about it in adult terms. When you feel like your partner hasn't heard you, one of two things may happen. Either you internalize your frustration, or you pick at your partner until you can express yourself with a fight. Children are no different. They're just using a child's resource to express that they don't feel heard—they're using whining.

Saying, "Use your words" simply causes a child to rephrase a whiney request, but the whining rarely stops. That's why parents have to repeat, "Use your words" so often. "Use your words" doesn't teach a child what she needs to know in order to manage the big feelings that caused the whining in the first place. It actually frustrates the child and causes the whining to come full circle again.

Whining is a signal a child's uses to tell you she's having trouble managing a situation or her feelings. Saying "Use your words," can make her feel as if you've pushed her away, instead of listening to the only signal she can provide at the moment. If the signal goes unnoticed, either she'll whine again or moves on to a stronger way to express herself, like screaming or throwing a tantrum.

An important first step to help reduce whining is to teach your child to express her feelings instead of whining. You might say, "Sweetie, I hear a whiny voice. Can you tell me what you're feeling instead of using the whiny sound please?" That's clearer information for a child to follow than saying, "Use your words."

Helping a child locate what she's feeling does many things. It shows her she's heard. It stops a power struggle or a tantrum from being the resource she uses to express herself. It helps her locate what's she's feeling and express it so she doesn't stuff her feelings. And best of all, it stops the whining noise!

Quick View

- The first step to help reduce whining is to notice. Instead of tuning out whining, realize whining is what your child is using to tell you she's having trouble.
- The second step is to teach a child to express her feelings instead of whine.
- Only saying, "Use your words" doesn't teach a child what she needs to know to manage her big feelings.
- Try, "I hear a whiny voice. Can you tell me what you're feeling in a regular voice instead of using the whiny voice?"

CHAPTER

4

FRUSTRATION

32. A Playroom ~ In the Garage?

This idea came from a client of mine in Portland, Oregon, where it rains a lot! When parents and children are trapped in the house all day due to weather, they can seriously get on one another's nerves. Did you know there's a playroom in your house that you didn't know you had? This magical room is just waiting for you, if you do a little cleaning first. It's your garage!

Clean out the garage, making sure all dangerous chemicals and tools are locked away so your child, and the neighborhood kids, can't climb up and investigate what's in the bright orange bottle. This is a great opportunity to recycle, or maybe even get a small shed to lock up any tools, machines or poisons. If your laundry area is in the garage, it is absolutely necessary that you lock up the detergents, lock the washer and dryer, and be with the children *100% of the time*. Okay, enough of my warnings. You understand how many dangers are lurking in the garage.

After cleaning the garage, get some blue painter's tape and divide the cleaned space into four or more sections. Each section creates a different zone so several activities can happen simultaneously.

Here are some ideas of what to do in each zone:

- Using the blue painter's tape, create a bike track so the kids can ride around and around without interrupting a sibling who's doing something else.
- One zone can be a mini basketball court.
- One zone can have a table for crafts. Load up a rolling cart with craft supplies and you're all ready to go.
- One zone can have large blocks in it.
- Use empty boxes so the kids can create clubhouses, caves and castles.

- Use blue painter's tape and create a railroad track for toy trains.
- Get different sized boxes and tubes to create an obstacle course. Carpet stores and big box stores will have different shapes and sizes of boxes and tubes that they may let you have.
- One section can be a stage, all set-up with costumes, and props for plays.

If you can afford it, use carpet squares or big interlocking mat pads (I found them at Sam's) to put on the floor so nobody hurts his or her head if they fall. You can also use a couple of layers of big boxes stuffed with blankets taped to the floor to break a fall.

Quick View

- Clean out the garage, making sure all dangerous chemicals and tools are locked away.
- Get some blue painter's tape and divide the space into four or more sections.
- Use carpet squares, big interlocking mat pads, or home-made padding to protect against any possible falls.

33. Band-Aid Phase ~ Giving It Back

There comes a time, around age four or five, when every little scratch a child gets requires a band-aid. A lot of parents will say, "Relax, it's just a tiny scratch" or "Stop being a baby; you're not getting a band-aid." or "They're expensive. Stop making such a fuss!" and so on. There is another way to handle this phase, and it doesn't cost a thing. It's called *Giving It Back*.

How to Give It Back: The idea here is to have the child return to the place where he hurt himself and give the pain back. This gives the child something to focus on instead of the need for a band-aid. You will need to model this for your child so he can see that this is what people do when they get hurt.

Use stubbing your toe as an example. Pretend to stub your toe. Go back to the exact spot on the furniture where you did the damage and put the injured part of your toe up to that spot. Say out loud to the furniture, "I'm sorry I bumped into you. Please take the pain away." Because children still believe in magic, this looks and sounds doable to her. You'll be amazed at how quickly you can encourage her to do the same thing.

Warning: One time my kids were playing in the bathroom and the older one went to slam the younger one's hand on the counter. The younger one quickly moved his hand out of the way and the older one hit his finger on the counter instead. He screamed and I went running. I went in and saw no blood, no scratch and he was able to bend it. So I said, "You're okay. Please apologize for trying to hit your brother's finger, and let's go back to playing." That seemed to be the end of it, until the next morning when he woke up and screamed because his finger was black. He'd broken it and I didn't catch it. Oh, did I feel like a horrible mother! So, please learn from me and make sure to really check the wound before you try this little tip.

Quick View

- Have the child return to the place where he hurt himself and give the pain back.
- Put the injured part of your toe up to that spot.
- Say out loud to the furniture, "I'm sorry I bumped into you. Please take the pain away."

34. "Yuck" ~ Conquering Food Avoidance

We've all given our children something new to taste, only to have them push it away saying, "Yuck, I hate it." It's at that moment when most parents will do one of three things. Some parents will argue with, or try to persuade, their child to change his mind about the food. Some will insist the child eat the food, like it or not. Others decide this food is simply something their child doesn't like and add it to a growing list of other foods the child hates, making it more and more difficult to cook one meal for the entire family.

The truth is that most children need seven to ten exposures to a new food before they're willing to begin to accept it. There is a way to expose your child to a new food enough times for them to be willing to eat it without an argument, and it's easier than you think. I won't lie here. It's highly likely that the first seven to ten times you enforce this new rule you will still hear, "Yuck, I hate it." Don't let that stop you. Simply maintain the attitude, "You're welcome to hate the food, and a rule is a rule." That may make things a bit easier.

A wonderful book called, *Night of the Veggie Monster* by George McClements outlines a non-negotiable, yet tolerable, way for children to slowly introduce their palate to the taste of different foods. You can also do a "palate test." Choose a dish and make it three ways, bland, normal and spicy. Let your child choose which version they like best. My oldest, a very picky eater as a child, shocked us when he chose the spicy version of most foods!

A "Thank You Bite" provides a child with the seven to ten exposures they need to begin to get their taste buds used to the food. The key to accomplishing a "Thank You Bite" without an argument is to cut the food into several different sizes, each one fairly *small*. If you make the bites big, hoping to sneak the food into your child, you'll have an argument on your hands. Have your child choose which smallish bite *they* want to eat. Make sure you accept that choice without comment, which gives your child some power in a situation where you usually make all the decisions.

Don't forget the power of dipping sauces. This worked beautifully for my kids. I allowed them to choose a sauce to dip their food in each time they had to take a "Thank You Bite." One child loved cheese on everything, and the other came to love barbecue sauce on everything. Who knew?

Quick View

- Thank You Bites provide a child with the seven to ten exposures they need to get used to new food.
- Cut the food into several different sizes, each one fairly *small*.
- Have your child choose which smallish bite *they* want to eat.
- Don't forget the power of dipping sauces.

35. "Don't Get Out of Bed!" ~ Try This

Rituals are not just for calming a child down; they can also be used to help your child stay in bed. Rituals work on the subconscious level to nonverbally remind a child of what you want them to know. Here are a few ideas to help keep a child in her room once you say "Good night."

Music: Many preschools successfully use music to create a quiet environment for resting. The music is turned on as the kids are going potty to non-verbally remind them to quiet down and use hushed voices. You can achieve that same non-verbal reminder by putting music on while you read stories. Quiet classical music works well, and can stay on after you leave, to create safety, consistency and comfort. Use a child's CD player, or a fairly simple indestructible player of some kind, so your child can restart the music in the middle of the night if need be. Make sure to tape off the volume control so it can't be turned up, and clearly mark the play button so she knows how to turn it on without you.

Lighting: Consider putting a rheostat on the light switch to adjust the lighting in your child's room, or use a lamp with a low-watt bulb while reading. A darker setting sends a message to your child that it's time to settle down and go to sleep. Some children must have a night-light, and that's fine. The truth is, however, that no light is better for a good night's sleep. To transition a child from a night light to no lights, teach her how she can see in the dark.

Falling Asleep: Trying to figure out *how* to make yourself go to sleep can actually cause agitation, resulting in a child getting up or calling for you. Tell her that she has to be quiet and *stay in bed,* but she doesn't have to fall asleep until she's ready. This changes things for her. Yes, she'll sing quietly, thrash about, talk to her stuffed animals, but sooner rather than later, she'll finally get tired, bored and fall asleep—and you'll get an evening to yourselves!

Forgive Me: I can't remember which blog this tip came from. Try a get-out-of-bed-once pass, good for one trip out of bed. Because of the pass, you'll be expecting her to get out of bed, which allows you to remain calm instead of frustrated. It will probably take a night or two for your child to realize that she needs to save the pass for a time when she really wants you, instead of wasting it on something silly, but she'll get there. Some kids actually stay in bed, debating when to use the pass, and fall asleep in the process. What could be better than that?

Quick View

- Music is a great non-verbal way to send the signal it's time to settle down.
- Turn off some lamps in the house as the day winds down. Use a lower watt bulb to read stories at night.
- Tell a child that they have to stay in bed, but don't have to fall asleep.
- Consider a get-out-of-bed-once pass.

36. End of the Day ~ "Play With Me"

Dr. T. Berry Brazelton coined the phrase "Pulling into the Break-Down Lane," when he referred to the end-of-the-day neediness. Let's face it, you're tired, your child is tired, and, if you're a working parent, your child wants to spend time with you. The end of the day always causes a rush to make dinner, because we all know if you don't eat on time, bedtime will be late, and will take time away from what's left of your evening. When you pile all of that up and sprinkle it with "Hold me" or "Spend time with me," it can cause any parent to come close to the edge!

Try combining what you have to do with spending time with your child to make the end of the day less frustrating and chaotic. Perhaps one of these ideas will help.

For the younger child who wants to be held, try this. "I will hold you until the timer rings. Then I'll pull your chair into the kitchen so I can walk by and kiss you as you stay seated and play while I cook. If you throw things off the table, you'll have to go play in another room, because toys on the floor aren't safe when hot food is cooking."

For the slightly older child who wants to be near you, try this. "You can get four toys and climb under the kitchen table and play far away from the hot stove, and we can talk while I cook. But if you come out from under the table you'll have to play in the playroom, away from the hot food."

For the child who is older still, try this invitation. "Sweetie, I miss you when you're in school. I'd like to offer you a special invitation. I was wondering if you'd like to join me in the kitchen for a little while. I can make dinner, and we can catch-up on things. Then, you can go do your homework. But, if you fool around, instead of doing homework, we won't be able to visit first tomorrow. What do you say?"

This works well because you're spending time with your child and not feeling as if you have to push him away because of all the end of the day things you have to accomplish. And your child gets his empty tank filled up with some attention. You've already clearly stated what will happen if he doesn't follow the rules, which makes it really easy to skip negotiations and go right to asking him to play elsewhere. When he naturally feels filled up with your attention, or becomes bored, he'll go play. He feels loved and you aren't frustrated, and that's a good thing.

Quick View

- To help avoid end-of-the-day neediness, consider doing the opposite of "go play." Invite your child to join you.
- A young child can stay seated and play while you cook. If she throws toys, she has to play elsewhere for a few minutes and then can come back and try again. To learn more about the concept of "Try Again" see tip #57.
- A slightly older child can get four toys and climb under the kitchen table to play.
- An older child can join you at the kitchen table and chat before or while doing homework.

37. "How Was School?" ~ And Don't Say "Fine"

Every day at 3:00 p.m., parents pick up kids and ask the same question: "How was school today?" And every day children say, "Fine!" And every day parents wonder, is there something she doesn't want to tell me? Is everything really okay? Of course, some children tell their parents so much about their day that the parent can't imagine what it would be like to have a child who simply answers "fine" when asked how the day went.

The truth is children do not have the give and take of social interaction down yet. They need practice to learn how to share when asked questions that don't have obvious answers. For them school *was* fine and nothing happened that made it *not fine*. As a child gets older they may be hiding behind the word "fine" but kids ages one through seven usually mean, "Yup, school was fine."

Another way to get more information from your child is to change the question you ask. Try one of these conversation starters.

- "What was the funniest or weirdest thing you heard today?"
- "Who brought the best or smelliest food?"
- "Who was the nicest or the meanest person today?"

This opens up a conversation quickly; you'll be amazed at what comes out! It will be probably more than you wanted to hear!

Quick View

- Creating a habit of asking different after-school questions, like the ones above, inspires conversation.
- Asking questions like this teaches a child how to share their day and allows you to learn more about who they are.

38. Hush ~ Can't You See I'm Talking

I've seen lots of parents who think part of parenting is stopping adult conversations so they can *fully address* a child who has interrupted them. The problem with that is what the child learns from that. She learns that adults in my life stop what they're doing to address my needs. The world doesn't work that way.

It's okay to ask your child to please be quiet. It's how you ask for quiet that holds the key. If you ignore her or let her talk without end, you'll probably get to a point where you can't take it anymore and yell, "Enough" or even "Shut up."

Instead of blurting out hurtful words, create a boundary using words that briefly explain I will not be interrupted at this time. You could say:

- "This conversation is for adults. Stand here silently or go back to fun. What will you do?"
- "I am talking right now. What do you need to do?"
- "My ears are listening to an adult right now. Would you like crayons or a tape recorder to tell your story?"

Teach her a signal that she can use if it's an emergency, so she always has the ability to inform you if there's trouble. Those responses not only handle the interruption, they also teach her about the give-and-take of conversation in social situations.

Quick View

- Don't wait until you're fed up to ask for quiet or it may come out as a harsh reaction.
- Asking for quiet teaches her that she's not always the center of attention, and the give-and-take of conversation.

39. Inside Voice ~ Take It Down a Notch

Children find it easy to forget that crossing the threshold into the house means it's time to calm down and use inside voices; they're having too much fun! Many tips and ideas abound to help children go from using an outside voice to an inside voice. Here are two more.

With younger children, try using a step-down method. Take your child outside to a set of stairs and have him move down one step. Then ask him, "Did you go up or down?" After he says "down," ask him to show you what he thinks his voice would sound like if you asked him to take his voice down by a step before he came inside. Tell him from now on, when he comes up to a door from the outside, he needs to take his voice down by one step before entering.

The next time he comes in having forgotten to use an inside voice, you can say, "Wow, that's a powerful outside voice. I need you to lower your voice by one step." Keep asking him to lower his voice step by step until he reaches what you consider an acceptable level in your house. Using the image of a step reminds him which direction you want his voice to go.

For an older child, who really knows the rules, try this. When your child comes bursting in from outside, too wild to remember to use his inside voice say, "Freeze. What do you need to do before you take another step?" Saying "freeze" tells him he has to stay glued to that spot until he figures out what he needs to do: "lower his voice."

An added benefit for both age groups in activating an inside voice this way is it brings the energy level down from outside play mode to inside calm mode.

Quick View

- Take your child outside to a set of stairs and have him move down one step. Ask him, "Did you go up or down?"
- Have him show you what his voice sounds like when asked to take his voice down by one step.
- Tell him from now on, when he arrives at a door from the outside, he needs to take his voice down by one step.
- When an older child comes bursting in from outside with a loud outside voice say, "Freeze."

40. Modeling ~ This Isn't "Project Runway"

Most children don't really know how to deal with frustration. That's one reason why they yell, fight with siblings, have meltdowns, say mean words, take toys, hit someone, and so on. They're frustrated that they can't have what they want, when they want it.

You don't have to wait for a time when your child is frustrated in order to teach him or her how to handle frustration; you can be proactive. Since children are always watching you, even when you don't think they are, show them how to manage frustration by modeling how *you* deal with things when *you're* frustrated.

Make up a situation that would frustrate you, like running out of an ingredient when you're cooking. Don't make a big deal out of it; just pretend your children aren't listening or watching, and show them how you deal with a frustrating situation. Go ahead and act as if you're about to get really frustrated, then take a deep breath, and say out loud, "Okay, let me think about what I can do instead," and then do it.

You'll be amazed at how quickly they'll repeat the methods you used to deal with their own frustration.

Quick View

- Frustration is one of the top ingredients for fights, tantrums and power struggles.
- Be proactive. Use the fact that you're the best role model your child can have to demonstrate the behavior you want him to learn.
- Create a situation that allows you to pretend that you're frustrated. Then model how to go from frustration to taking a deep breath and to looking for a solution, instead of getting upset.

41. Practicing Reading ~ Easy and Fun?

All parents hope their children will love the adventures they find in books and choose to read them often. In order to learn to read, children need to read out loud as often as possible. Many teachers assign a half hour of reading aloud several times a week. Some children can't wait to show off how well they read. For others, reading aloud is filled with hesitancy and dread. They may feel overwhelmed, embarrassed or criticized.

If that's the case for your child, have him read aloud to a dog, a cat, a doll or a sibling. When I was little and learning to read, I read to my younger sister every day after school. Because she'd gotten so much exposure to letters and words, she was reading before she went to kindergarten.

Terry Doherty, of TheReadingTub.com, gave me a great suggestion to help get kids to read. She recommends that you let children read *anything* they want, from cereal boxes to video game instructions to books about dolls or race cars...anything. After all, it's all reading!

Quick View

- If your child seems uncomfortable about having you listen to him read, let him read to a dog, a cat or a doll while you listen from another room.
- Let your children read anything they want, including cereal boxes, video game descriptions and directions, anything they see that captures their attention and encourages reading.

42. Relaxing ~ Try Giving to Get Some

Every parent longs for a bit of private time at the end of the day, and can't just announce, "I'm taking 30 minutes off" and get away with it. In most homes, if a parent tries to have some private time, the kids go looking for Mom or Dad or create a problem requiring that they to come and deal with something. Here's how you can get 30 minutes of uninterrupted time—but you have to give to get. This works for working *and* stay-at-home parents.

What you give: The key to getting *uninterrupted* time is to give the children some one-on-one time *first.*

Part One: Build excitement by telling the kids that they get to decide what they want to read or play during mini-playtime. Working parents can do this in the morning before work. Stay-at-home parents can do it just before a scheduled mini-playtime. It's good to call it mini-playtime, so the kids won't be expecting you to spend a bunch of time with them. Working parents: make sure to have a snack waiting in the car when you pick the kids up from daycare so you can go directly to mini-playtime when you walk in the door.

Part Two: Don't look at email, or your phone before or during mini-play time. Not answering messages or calls tells your child that you're truly focused on him and that he's important to you.

Part Three: Set the timer, and really play with the kids for about 20 minutes. That's the key. Children feel it when you *really* play with them. Getting filled up with a parent's "full" attention *before* the parent attempts private time is what makes this work.

Part Four: When the timer goes off, and mini-playtime is over is when you ask them what video they want to watch. This is the best time of the day to use a video—when it works for you! Make sure *not* to say, "Leave me alone while the video is on." That will only remind them you're going away again, causing them to come find you.

What you get: 30 minutes of *uninterrupted* time for yourself while they watch the video.

Some parents say, "I already pop in a video and get 30 minutes to myself. What's the big deal?" The key is 30 minutes of *uninterrupted* time. If you just walk in and start a video, the kids will get up every few minutes to find you, since they haven't seen you all day. By fully focusing on them during mini-playtime, before private time, you're filling them up with enough attention to *buy* you 30 minutes of *uninterrupted* time. Stay-at-home parents tell me they use video time to catch-up on housework, emails or whatever. But that means there's never a time in the day when you get to just relax and refuel.

Most reactions from parents happen because the parent hasn't refueled. They're stretched past their capacity, tired, and possibly resentful. Giving yourself 30 minutes every day to rest, read, lie down or do something relaxing, makes you more capable of doing the second shift without yelling and punishing.

Quick View

- Create excitement by talking about today's mini-playtime.
- Don't look at email, phone or messages, before or during mini-playtime.
- Create a mini-playtime for about 20 minutes, and really focus on the kids.
- After focusing on the children during mini-playtime, ask them what video *they* want to watch while you have *private* time.

43. Talking Too Loud ~ 4 Voices

When a child goes from an outside to an inside voice, the change is usually only temporary. Before you know it, he's loud again. I think one reason this happens is that he doesn't know just how loud he sounds. You can help him learn by showing him that he actually has four levels of sound, or four voices he can use, instead of just one loud voice.

Get a children's tape recorder and record him using his outside voice, his inside voice, a voice that's in between the outside and inside voice, and record him using a whisper.

The in-between voice can be used to remind him that he's almost reached his inside voice, but not quite yet. The whisper voice will teach him what kind of voice to use when someone is sleeping, or working quietly.

Make sure to identify situations when he's supposed to use a certain or voice so he knows what you expect. Also, let him practice by having access to the tape recorder so he can listen as many times as he likes. See if that makes any difference, and as my grandmother said, "It couldn't hurt!"

Quick View

- Most children think there is only one level of voice: *loud*.
- Introduce four different levels of sound a child can copy, outside, inside, in between the two and a whisper.
- Use a tape recorder and record the child using words at each level. Let him practice them so you can request one of the four voices when needed.

44. Thank You Notes ~ Be Proactive

The old saying goes, "If you want something done right, do it yourself." Such is the case, most of the time, when it comes to sending "thank you" notes or emails. This tip changes that old saying to, "If you want something done, that you know your child will resist doing, be proactive." What do I mean?

We've all known what it's like when a birthday or holiday is over and it's time to send "thank you" notes or emails. It's a complaint-fest every time. To change that from a power struggle to a fun project, do the "thank you" notes or emails before the big event and capitalize on the excitement of the upcoming birthday or holiday.

Make it easy on yourself by creating the body of one "thank you" note on the computer, making sure to leave spaces for the person's name and the gift they gave. Compose a few "thank you" notes each night so the child isn't being forced. This also allows you to talk about the upcoming party and lets the excitement begin!

By being proactive, you've infused a dreaded chore with anticipation, excitement, one-on-one time with a parent, and created memories. And it's all done before the big day occurs.

Quick View

- About a week before a birthday or a holiday, have your child join you at the computer.
- Create a list of those who you think will be giving gifts.
- Have child dictate the "thank you" note so it actually sounds like him. Resist making corrections if you can.
- Make sure to leave a blank space for the gift and who the letter will be addressed too.
- Do a few each night and turn a dreaded chore into a fun project!

45. Time for Bed ~ Leaving the Fun

Most parents are as tired as their children are when it's bedtime. That means they may be forgetting some really good ideas that can make bedtime a little easier. Here are some tips that you may or may not know.

Children need a brief cool down period after active play or TV time, about 30 to 40 minutes, in order to get sleepy enough to fall asleep. That means no more tickle-fests or running around before bedtime. If Dad tends to come home late and wants to play with the kids, he may need to rethink the way he spends time with them. Let Dad be in charge of calming them down, not getting them wound up. Let Dad play calm games, read, do bath or bedtime.

When a parent says, "Time for bed," he knows that it really means the bedtime "process" has begun. When a child hears "Time for bed," she thinks it means bedtime is right at this moment, so she tends to resist. What if you said, "It's get-ready time" instead? That way the child realizes that she still has some time left with Mommy and Daddy before bedtime.

Most sleep experts suggest using the same routine every night before bed. The routine not only works to reduce resistance to bedtime, it also allows a child to settle down, step by step, by performing the same activities in the same order each night.

Here's a good routine to use as a baseline to create your routine each night.

- Move from active to calm activities one hour before bed.
- Take a short walk after dinner to release any pent-up energy before bath time.

- Run a warm bath and put ¼ cup of table salt in it to dissolve. The magnesium in the salt removes tension from muscles and relaxes the body.
- Add some *Gerber's Lavender Baby Wash* to the salt water too. It doesn't matter that the product says it's for babies; it works well for older children too. Lavender is powerful aromatherapy and really does help you sleep well. I wouldn't suggest using the essential oil with children. It's probably too strong.
- Encouraging sleepiness: Follow bath time with a glass of warm milk and use cinnamon instead of sweetener.
- Turn the lights down about 30 minutes before bed. Either put your lights on a rheostat or change the bulbs to three-way bulbs.
- Of course, read bedtime stories.
- Don't forget, to a child, bedtime means "I have to leave the fun," and no child wants to do that!

Quick View

- No roughhousing if it's 30–40 minutes before bed.
- Curtail TV about 30 minutes before bed too, unless your child has no problems in that area.
- Change the words from "time for bed" to "it's get-ready time."
- Using a routine sends subliminal messages a child's body to begin to get sleepy.

46. Tired of Reminding ~ Use Visual Clues

If a parent looks for it, they can always find something about their child or their behavior to correct. Parents do need to teach, correct and prepare a child for life. The big question is *how*?

How would you feel if you were corrected for every little thing, 20 to 30 times a day? Think about how you'd feel if your husband or wife spent the entire day picking at every little thing you did. Would you be motivated to change? Possibly you'd have a deep, rumbling anger waiting to erupt at some point towards whomever is doing the correcting. Children are no different. They're just miniature versions of us.

There is a way to correct behavior without picking on every little thing. This tip shows you that *how* you present the information is the most important part.

Does your child pull off far more toilet paper than he needs? Instead of warning and threatening each time he goes potty, empower him to do it himself!

- Place a piece of blue painter's tape on the wall. Tell him, "When the top of the toilet paper reaches the top of the blue line rip it off." That allows him to measure the toilet paper out himself, instead of reminding him.
- The same concept works for washing hands. Does your child turn the faucet handle on farther than it needs to be, causing water to go everywhere? Place a piece of painter's tape where you want the handle to stop turning so the right amount of water comes out. This visual mark gives the child all the information she needs to wash her hands herself, without all the reminders.

When you look at a situation through a child's eyes, you can see all the steps needed for how to be successful. Using blue tape or any visual method allows you to leave clear, age-appropriate clues so he can be responsible for cleaning up his own mess.

Quick View

- When parents look at situations through a child's eyes they can see all the age-appropriate steps.
- To stop reminding a child of how to do something, use step-by-step visual clues so the child can manage things for themselves, including clean-up if need be.

47. Walking Rules ~ Fun for All

It's no fun to go out on a walk with your child when you're spending the entire time correcting her for running ahead of you. You know that she's too young to see any danger, so you warn her constantly, but she feels like she's being controlled and acts like a horse chomping at the bit to get away.

Here's an idea to help both parent and child get what they need when they're out on a walk. The child gets to experience her freedom, and the parent gets to have rules and boundaries so he feels safer when approaching potential danger.

You're going to teach your child that there are two kinds of walks: an "I can touch you walk" and a "free walk." One is for walking where there are cars, and the other is for places where there are no cars. The best place to learn about and practice these walks is an empty parking lot or an unused road.

Where there are cars: Most children want to walk without holding their parent's hand, so that becomes the prize and the consequence. Tell your child she can walk *without* holding hands, as long as she walks close enough for you to reach out and touch her shoulder. However, if she gets too far ahead and you can't easily touch her shoulder, she has to *hold your hand for a count of 20,* and then she can try again.

Details: If a parent has to lean forward by one or two steps in order to bring the child to safety, she may not make it in time. Have your child walk no farther in front of you than a semi-outstretched arm. Then, if you need to grab her, all you do is fully extend your arm, grab her and bring her to safety. Make sure to use positive reinforcement too. Reach out several times during the walk, tap her on the shoulder and say, "Look I can touch your shoulder. Thanks for walking this way."

Where there are no cars: Being out in nature is a great way to relax, unless you're constantly warning your child to stay close. Here again, you want to teach this in a controlled environment. Once mastered, you can move the fun to a trail, park or campground.

Again, the prize is *not* holding the parents hand, and the consequence *is* holding the parent's hand. Tell her, "You can walk without holding my hand as long as you go no farther than the tree branch where I hung my hat up the road," or whatever marker you choose. Make sure to go up and touch the branch you're talking about so you know for a fact that your child understands where she must stop. Tell her she can walk fast or slow, it's up to her, but when she gets to the boundary, she must wait or come running back to you. It's important that she knows she's not allowed to go past the agreed marker, or she'll start inching farther away to test the boundary and that could be dangerous. If she does anything that she isn't supposed to do, you'll hold her hand for a count of 20, and then she can try again.

A free walk allows her to experience freedom and responsibility at the same time. When a child is entrusted with being responsible for her own safety, she tends to stay closer than you would think.

Teaching your child walking rules allows you both to feel safer, whether you're in the city or the country, and that gives you the freedom to have fun!

Quick View

- Holding, or not holding a parent's hand is the prize or the consequence, doesn't matter if it's a city or country walk.
- When there are cars, teach your child to walk no farther in front of you than a semi-outstretched arm.
- When there are no cars, create a marker to show the child where to stop, and let her be responsible for herself.

48. "Why'd You Do That?" ~ "I Dunno"

How many times have you said, "Why'd you do that?" and gotten a sheepish look and a quiet, "I dunno." I looked up "dunno" in the Urban Dictionary, it said, "Means 'I don't know.'" Contrary to popular belief, it does not mean "Keep asking me the same question and maybe an answer will pop up." That's what this tip is about.

More often than not, demanding an answer when you first encounter a problem will only cause a child to withdraw to protect herself from her angry parents. A child knows she's been caught, and is upset and fearful of what's coming next. To be grilled about why she did something may be more than she can handle at that moment.

In order to win cooperation and gain resolution, consider asking questions.

- "Is this okay in our house?"
- "What were you trying to do?"
- "What do you need to do to fix this?"
- "Are you allowed to take this?"
- "Do we do things without Mom's or Dad's help?"

Those questions allow you to skip over why she did what she did for the moment, and get directly to what the rules are. After directing her toward resolving whatever happened you can explore why she did what she did.

Quick View

- Demanding an answer when you first encounter an issue will only cause a child to withdraw.
- The child knows she's been caught, and is upset and fearful of what's coming next. Try asking questions instead.

CHAPTER

5

GRANDPARENTS

49. Contact by Phone ~ Meeting the Face

These days, with cell phones and email, grandparents and grandchildren really are able to stay connected. Technology can present a problem though. Suppose the grandparents are coming to meet their grandchild in person for the first time. Your child, however, is one who's pretty shy around new people. The conflict is you don't want to force your child to warm-up to someone she only knows from phone calls but hasn't met in person yet. And you don't want the grandparents to be upset by her shyness, and possible rejection of them. What can you do? Here's a sweet techie way to help the child match the phone voice with the face.

Have Grandma and Grandpa call the child on the phone when they're either about five minutes away from the house or as they're walking down the corridor from the plane. As the grandparents talk to grandchild have them decide what signal the grandparents will use so the grandchild will recognize them when they see each other.

Have the grandparent remain on the phone until he's standing in front of his grandchild. This allows the grandchild to see, with her own eyes, that the voice she loves on the phone is also the voice coming from the person standing in front of her. Now the fun can begin!

Quick View

- Have grandma and grandpa call the child on the phone when they're either about five minutes away from the house or as they're walking down the corridor from the plane.
- Choose a signal the grandparents will use so the grandchild will recognize them when they see each other.

50. Things To Do ~ Family Bonding

When grandparents don't live close by, the time they spend with their grandchildren is precious. They may come into town ready to spend lots of time with their grandchild, only to be met by someone who doesn't remember them or who is timid in the beginning. Here are a few tips to warm things up and get the fun started.

Before the grandparent leaves home, Mom and Dad can send them a current list of what the kids like and dislike, such as their favorite breakfast, favorite ice cream, a movie they want to see in the theater, favorite museum, and, of course, favorite books. This way, the grandparent always seems to hit a home run when they're suggesting things to do.

The grandparents can send each grandchild an exclusive invitation through snail mail, or email and invite him or her to spend some one-on-one time with them when they come to town. Children love getting mail and a private invitation makes things that much more special.

Mom can put several of her child's favorite books on hold at the library so the grandparent and grandchild can make a special trip there and check out some books. This creates wonderful memories and extra cuddle time.

To warm things up even more, create a question-and-answer party over ice cream. The child gets to ask the grandparent anything they want to know about their parent's or their parent's childhood.

The grandparent can bring a favorite recipe from the parent's childhood and invite her grandchild to help her cook it and serve it to Mommy and Daddy.

The grandparent can take his or her grandchild to the nursery and buy a small tree to come home and plant. This gives the grandparents something to talk about with the grandchild after they go home.

Doing these kinds of things, instead of just bringing a gift, creates rituals your grandchild will be excited to repeat each time you visit, and will remember for years to come.

Quick View

- Before their arrival, send a list of favorite breakfast foods, museums, movies and books to the grandparents.
- Have grandparents send a special invitation to each child, inviting them to spend some special one-on-one time together.
- Create a Q&A party over ice cream so grandparent and grandchild can get to know each other.
- Have favorite books on hold at the library.
- Go to the nursery and buy a small tree to plant so there's a built-in conversation-starter during phone calls.

51. Watching the Kids ~ Use My Rules

When a relative babysits, most parents feel the need to leave a list telling the relative what their child is used to. Things like, all wild play stops at 7:30, then she bathes, then we read, etc, so the child feels really comfortable while the parents are gone. But, giving an experienced relative a list like that could offend them.

Instead of framing it so it sounds like you don't trust them, tell them you're giving them this list because you need to be able to relax. You could say, "I know you don't need any instructions, you've raised three wonderful children already. I'm doing this for *my* benefit, so *I* can feel like a good parent and relax while I'm away." Saying something like that allows you to send the information without offending anyone.

Just know one thing: They *will* think you're crazy, and will most likely do things their way while you're gone. But you get to relax, knowing that if something does happen, you've left instructions about the way you do things, just in case.

Final note: We've all heard a flight attendant say, "Parents, please put your oxygen mask on first so you have enough oxygen to care for your child." Parenting requires that you have the energy you need in order to do the job, too. Planning a little getaway doesn't make you a bad parent; it makes you more rested, so you're more able to handle the daily rigors of parenting.

Quick View

- Instead of insisting that relatives follow *your* rules when they watch your kids, tell them you need to leave a list of what your child is used to so *you* can relax.
- Know that they will probably do things their own way, but your list will be there if needed.

CHAPTER

6

LEARNING

52. Mistakes ~ *Really* Think About It

When a child makes a big mistake, most parents really want their child to understand the gravity of the situation, and rightfully so. Some parents begin to lecture, to make sure their child knows how bad it is. Others hand down a huge punishment so she'll never forget what she did. Some parents feel their child's behavior is a reflection on them, and make decisions about what to do from that place of embarrassment. Still others are just plain angry, and remain so as a way to punish their child.

I'm not here to tell you how to handle situations with your child. You're the parent and you know what's best. I do want to point out that most children are so upset at being caught that they can't *really think*. *Really thinking* about what happened, what to do to make sure it never happens again, and how to fix it, are what will help ensure that it doesn't happen again.

Think back to when you were little. Most of us were yelled at, and the yelling caused us to fear or resent our parents. It didn't make us *really think* about the situation. We'd promise just about anything we thought our parents wanted to hear so we could get it over with.

Many parents have told me that, when they were little, what *did* make an impression on them was when their parents said they were disappointed. I'm not advocating that you tell your child you're disappointed in her. I'm advocating that you change your method to include teaching words. You'll still make an impression, your child will still learn, and it will be done without any residual guilt.

To help a child *really learn* from mistakes, he/she needs to be allowed to feel the weight of the consequences of his/her choices and what it will take to fix things.

What if you said, "I'm pretty upset about this. You need to sit here and *really think* about what happened. When we talk later I want you to tell me what you will do differently next time so this doesn't happen again, how you plan to fix this, and what you think your consequence should be, if the situation calls for a consequence. Oh and by the way, *real thinking* isn't something that happens in five minutes. *Real thinking* can take a whole evening. Based on what you did, I'm guessing you'll be in here all evening. I'll check on you in a while to see what you have to tell me."

This sends the message that you're disappointed without needing to say it. It tells the child that it's her responsibility to figure out how to repair the damage she has caused. It creates a consequence, she has to stay in her room all night, or until you think she has given it enough thought. It allows you to remain calm so you can hug and love your child as they figure it all out.

I think that accomplishes just about everything you'd want from your child so she understands the gravity of a situation, don't you?

Quick View

- To create *real thinking,* allow a child to feel the weight of the consequences of his/her choices and what it will take to fix things.
- Have him sit in his room and think about what he will do differently next time, how he plans to fix things, and what his consequence should be, if the situation calls for a consequence.

53. Mistakes ~ Tender Teaching

It's obvious that you can't use the last tip when speaking to a younger child about a mistake. So what can you do to teach him about the mistake he just made?

First, it helps to realize that this may be the first time in his young life that your child has ever encountered the circumstances that surrounded the mistake. Even though the mistake may be a whopper, learning, much more than punishment, is what your child really needs now.

In order to teach your child about the mistake he made, you need to be aware of a few things.

- Young children tend to think the lecturing you do when they get into trouble is just another form of attention, even if you're yelling. To understand more on this topic read tip #17.

- When you yell at a young child to correct a mistake, you're focusing on only one side of the equation. You're only addressing what he *shouldn't* have done. You also need to address *what he should have done instead* because he's never encountered a situation like this before.

- Just like the older child, and even more so with a younger child, when fear, crying, or blaming is happening, any clear thinking you're asking him to do is pretty much impossible. A good way to deal with the situation, without overwhelming your child, is to ask him, "If you could re-do the situation how would it end?" Addressing the situation that way allows him to think about things using his imagination, which is on target for his age.

- When younger children become emotional, they have a more difficult time understanding adult language. It's helpful, when correcting behavior, to speak they way your child does, by using smaller words. This keeps the lines of communication open so you can get to the root of what caused the misbehavior. When the child is no longer emotional, you can go back to using adult words to increase his vocabulary.

His answer will tell you what his level of understanding is about the situation and show you what you need to teach him so he can learn from this mistake.

Quick View

- You can't use the big words when speaking to a younger child about a mistake.
- Remember, this may be the first time your child has encountered the circumstances that surround the mistake.
- Most parents tend to focus on only one side of the equation—what the child *shouldn't* have done. Parents also need to address what he *should have done instead.*

54. "Need to Go Potty?" ~ What He Hears

Sometimes the words we use, when talking to our children, undermine our intentions, and we don't even know it. Such is the case with potty training. Have you ever asked your child if he *needs* to go potty, he says "no", then pees on the floor? Or you ask him if he needs to go, only to see him do the "potty dance" too late to get him to the potty before he wets himself? Both situations can cause a parent to say, "Why didn't you tell me you had to go when I asked you?"

When words, potty training and developmental phases are mixed together in just the right way they can cause some confusion for a young child becoming skilled at using the toilet. Let me explain.

- A little one is still learning the English language as he begins the potty training process.
- He's just learning what the sensation feels like that tells him he *needs* to go potty.
- He's probably only two or three years old, and smack dab in the middle of the developmental phase where he's asserting his independence, which means his favorite word is "No!"

Children are what they call 'concrete learners", which means they focus on the exact meaning of words. When you ask him if he *needs* to go potty, he hears the word *needs* and decides, "I don't *need* to go potty, I *need* to keep playing." He automatically says "No," which also allows him to use the important word that Mom and Dad always use, and that makes him feel big and independent. And since he's just learning to respond to the sensation of needing to go pee, he ignores the feeling. Remember, being wet is okay with him; he's been wet since birth. *You* know that it feels better to be dry, but he's just learning about that.

So, what can you do? Begin by spending one to three days monitoring your child's natural rhythm, the times when he naturally goes to the bathroom each day. Don't say anything to him; just observe what his personal signals are. Is it the potty dance? Is it a wiggle, then staring off into the distance? Does he hide behind a chair because he wants privacy? What does he do? Write down the clues and times he naturally goes every day.

The day you choose to use the new words, start paying attention to him about five minutes before his natural time to go potty. Just before, or as soon as you see his potty clue, say in a firm, but excited, voice, "It's time to go potty—do you want to run to the potty or hold my hand?"

The way you phrase your question does several things.

- It tells him that it's time to go potty, and there are no choices.
- It allows him to feel independent, because *he decides* if he'll run or hold Mom's hand. That decision begins to fill his need for independence and can replace the automatic need to say "No."

When he's mastered potty training, you can go back to saying, "Do you need to go potty?" because he will fully know what the sensation feels like, and truly know if he needs to go or not.

Quick View

- Spend one to three days monitoring when your child naturally goes to the bathroom each day.
- Pay attention to your child about five minutes before his natural time to go potty.
- As soon as you see his clue, say in a firm, but excited voice, "It's time to go potty—do you want to run to the potty or hold my hand?"

CHAPTER

OUT IN PUBLIC

55. Begging for Stuff ~ Make It Stop

A nine-year-old boy is standing beside his mom in the checkout line desperately begging for a remote control car he's holding. He's whining as mom says, "No!" He gets louder and mom apologetically looks at the others in line and says, "No!" again. The boy repeatedly asks, "Why can't I have it? Why can't I have it?" Everyone in line witnesses the moment when mom caves in. She quietly says, "How much is it?" and the boy smiles.

Those "in the know" would advise mom to ignore him, or sternly remind him that behaving that way will *not* force her to buy the toy. It might even be suggested that he gets a time-out for behaving that way. However, those things won't change the *repeated* begging and whining intended to force a parent to make a purchase.

To truly make a change, look at the situation the way a child does. A parent's buying habits look like mom and dad get whatever they want, whenever they want it. A child misunderstands that and thinks he should have the same rights. He knows mom said "No!" but he still feels an overwhelming desire to have it, *now.*

Kids don't understand delayed gratification, saving for purchases, or how to manage any feelings that remain once they've been told "No!" Addressing your child's desire for the purchase is the key to shutting down begging and whining.

Here's what you can do.

Step One: Keep a small notebook for each of your children in your purse at all times.

Step Two: Instead of simply saying "No!" when your child asks for something, *excitedly* say, "I have your wish-book right here, do you want this to go on your birthday list or Christmas list?"

Step Three: Let her decide which list to add the item to and instantly write it down. This way she sees her desire for the toy has been recorded and she can let it go.

FYI: Remind her that the wish-book is for recording her wishes and does not guarantee she'll automatically receive everything on the list.

Step Four: What happens if she's still insisting on having it *now?* Since the purchase isn't a reward or a gift, why not use this as a teaching opportunity? Consider having her pay for half for the desired object so she learns about earning money, delaying gratification, math and decision-making. The sooner kids learn all that's involved in making a purchase, the less often they'll beg and whine for things. Who knows, she may even decide the toy isn't worth the effort needed to earn the money.

Quick View

- Carry a small notebook with you to record your child's wishes for things.
- Remind your child that recording wishes does not guarantee she'll receive everything on the list.
- Consider creating extra chores so your child can earn money to pay for 50% of an item when she has to have it *now.*

56. Communicating ~ The Silent Warning

Have you ever been uncomfortable, after you handled a situation in public, because your behavior was as intense as your child's? Wouldn't it be great if you had another way to correct your child's behavior in public without yelling? Well, it is possible, and that's what you'll learn in this tip.

Signals, gestures and one-word clues are great ways to let your child know that she's doing something she shouldn't be doing. This works as long as the signal, gesture or one-word clue isn't obviously pointing to the fact that she's being corrected. That means no finger shaking or clearing your throat or grabbing her arm or warning her. Using those kinds of signals alerts everyone around your child that she's misbehaving, and either causes them to encourage her to behave, or casts all eyes on both of you to see how things will turn out. Neither of you needs that kind of pressure or attention.

If you choose a one-word clue, pick a word that's unrelated to behavior, one that only you and your child know what it means. Using an unrelated word communicates respect to your child, and may increase the possibility that behavior changes more quickly. You can even whisper the one-word clue so no one hears. Perhaps something like, "caterpillar." An action can be as simple as pulling on your ear or rubbing your chin.

Choosing a signal, or a one-word clue, acts as a silent warning between you and your child, telling her, "I see you. Please stop what you're doing now, or I will have to do something." Make sure to have a conversation to explain what the signal means, and what will happen if she doesn't pay attention to the signal.

Using a signal allows a parent to remain calmer; the signal is doing the talking for her. The signal sends a message to the child that says, "I'm about to enforce the rules (or boundaries) that we have already discussed and I'm giving you a warning first to see if you can get it together. You decide whether you listen or I take action."

For a signal to work well, apply the signal one time. If nothing happens, go directly into action by standing up and doing what you said you would do. Using a signal is great for parents; it allows them to respond, not react to behavior. Using a clue, in combination with the next tip, #57, creates an unbeatable way to hand public misbehavior.

Quick View

- Choose a one-word clue. Pick a word that's unrelated to misbehavior, like "caterpillar."
- One-word clues are silent warnings that say, "I see you. Stop what you're doing or I'll have to do something.
- Apply a signal once. If nothing happens, go directly to correcting your child the way you normally would. This shows her that a signal is her one opportunity to change her behavior and avoid a correction.

57. Correcting ~ Right Here and Now

We've all seen it, either in the mall or in a restaurant. Dad looks embarrassed as his child misbehaves. He threatens his son under his breath, but it doesn't seem to be working. Dad looks around at the other adults with a look of apology, as if to say, "I'm sorry he's disturbing you!" It's a familiar scene; it's also one that can be avoided with some rehearsal.

Instead of going home to punish your child, try doing a shopping rehearsal. A rehearsal happens when a parent isn't in a hurry and doesn't have a shopping agenda. It allows you to respond calmly sending the message, "I mean business." Rehearsing tells a child what happens if he doesn't follow the rules, so there's no surprise when he's corrected right here, right now.

A rehearsal is not a one-time event. Think of the first few times you do this as a rehearsal for both of you. It can take time for a child to fully understand why you're leaving the store, and that he'll get the chance to try again. You need time to master this without reacting. Here are the three steps for doing a rehearsal.

Expectations. What are your expectations for public behavior? If your answer is, "He needs to behave," then go a little deeper. Think of your child as a blank slate that needs to have the details filled in. He needs to know what he's *supposed* to do, not just be told what you want him to *stop doing*. It's best to share your expectations in an age-appropriate way too: "I want you no more than three steps in front of me," or "Hands belong in pockets, but it's okay to look with your eyes."

Rehearsal Day. Pick a day when you're not in a hurry and have no shopping agenda. Go to a public place where your child regularly tends to misbehave, and wait for circumstances to unfold. Then, begin the correction.

The Correction. Before you get out of the car, announce your expectations, *and* what will happen if he doesn't cooperate. Say, "If you misbehave we'll leave the store and find a bench, where we'll sit until you've calmed down and can remember how you're supposed to behave. Then we'll go *back into the store* to *try again.*" The key here is the *going back to try again.* It shows him that no matter what, you're willing to stop what you're doing and correct him, if need be.

Some children only need this process to be repeated once. Others need to have this repeated several times before understanding what's going on. It's all with-in the range of normal.

P.S. If you have a cart full of food or merchandise when misbehavior shows up, just ask the manager to watch your cart until you return. Management is thrilled that you're doing something about the misbehavior and will support you any way they can! Also consider using a silent clue, tip #56, to warn your child before you leave the store. I think you'll find the combo an unbeatable way to handle behavior in public.

Quick View

- Let your child know the what the expectations are when you're in public.
- Rehearse this process on a day when you're not in a hurry and have no shopping agenda.
- Go to a public place where your child regularly tends to misbehave.
- Announce your expectations before you get out of the car.
- If he misbehaves, leave the store and sit on a bench until he's ready; then go back to the store and try again.
- Do this as many times as needed.

58. "Everyone's Staring!" ~ What to Say

Do you ever get the feeling that all eyes are on you when your child misbehaves in public? The truth is all eyes *are* on you, but probably not for the reason you think. Most parents think other people are looking at them and judging them as failures because their child is misbehaving.

I don't believe that's true. I think people begin by having empathy for you and then want to see if you're going to handle the situation. Onlookers want to see a parent in charge, not a child in charge. Personally, I never look. I figure parents have enough on their plates and don't need more glaring eyes.

If you feel you need to say something when you spot people looking, try saying, "Yes, we're having a moment." This statement usually satisfies all the gawkers. It tells onlookers that you know they're looking. It also tells them, "Yes, I'm aware that this is going on; I'm not ignoring it; I'm handling it in the best way I know how." A statement like that usually stops all the judgmental glances and turns them back into empathetic ones.

Quick View

- When you notice people gawking try using a simple statement like, "Yes we're having a moment."

- A statement like that tells onlookers that you are aware of the situation and doing the best you can.

- Saying, "Yes, we're having a moment." tends to turn most judgmental glances back into empathetic ones.

59. Cooperation ~ At a Restaurant?

For kids, going out to dinner can be lots of fun, or it can be overwhelming. Some children get wild from all the activity in a restaurant, while others feel lost in a sea of strange adults. No matter which type of child you have, a lot of waiting happens when you go out to dinner with the family.

Children have to wait to have the menus read to them, wait for water, wait for bread or crackers, wait for an adult to pay attention to them, wait to go to the bathroom, wait to talk and wait for food to arrive. That's a lot of waiting.

No matter how your child acts in a restaurant, every parent needs their child to listen to them. You have a better chance of having that happen if you use what I call rapid-fire questions. Rapid-fire questions have parents ask a bunch of questions really fast, one right after another, so the child has to listen closely in order to get any of the choices being offered.

What you'll notice about these rapid-fire questions is that they are also choices. Here are a few examples:

- "Do you want to sit next to Dad or Mom?"
- "Do you want a hotdog or chicken fingers?"
- "Would you like a puzzle or a coloring book now?"
- "Would you like water or milk?"
- "Would you like to eat this plain or do you want a dipping sauce?"
- "Do you want to go potty now or in five minutes?"
- "Would you like to go for a walk while we wait or would you prefer to color?"

It takes a lot of focus for a child to pay attention to all those questions. After answering all those questions the child may be ready to be quiet for a little while, allowing parents to possibly relax and enjoy having a minute or two to talk to each other.

Warning: This tip does *not* work for children who get stimulated by a lot of talking or activity.

Quick View

- Consider using rapid-fire questions when you first arrive at your table in a restaurant.
- Rapid-fire questions have parents ask a bunch of questions and present choices really fast, one right after another, so the child has to listen closely in order to get any of the choices being offered.
- *Warning:* This tip does *not* work for children who get stimulated by a lot of talking or activity.

CHAPTER

8

POWER STRUGGLES

60. "Do Not Argue!" ~ Who Goes First?

Power struggles are called many things—a fight, a battle of wills, or being challenged by your child. No matter what you call it, a power struggle occurs when two people are struggling to determine who has the power or control in a situation. Both people are yelling and/or arguing while trying to prove that their point of view is the right point of view. When you're in the middle of a power struggle, you know it. Power struggles are easy to get into, and hard to stop, unless you know the key.

This *Peanuts* cartoon perfectly illustrates how to get out of a power struggle once you're already involved in one. Lucy is yelling at Linus. Charlie Brown asks Linus, "Are you two fighting?" Linus answers, "She's fighting. I'm just sitting here."

I'm not suggesting you sit down and ignore your child, like Linus ignored Lucy. I'm suggesting you wait for the right moment to say what you need to say. When is the right moment? When your child has stopped talking. It sounds simple, and is extremely hard to do.

In order to stop a power struggle, you need to know how one unfolds first. A power struggle begins with a parental statement, followed by a child jumping in to argue against the parent's point. It's at that moment, when a parent gets totally sucked into the argument, and tries to stop things from going any further. The parent begins yelling, making corrections or threats, anything to stop things immediately. So how do you get out of a power struggle once it's begun? The parent stops talking first! Just stop talking and let your child keep talking until she notices that you've stopped.

The yelling that occurs during a power struggle, is the fuel that feeds the struggle, actually making the struggle grow. That's why you often hear parents say, "Things got out of control so quickly!" The key is to withdraw the fuel, to withdraw your portion of the yelling. Most parents think a child should stop yelling first. The truth is that parents are the role models, the child is still learning, and parent needs to stop yelling first.

The moment you stop participating in arguing, and your child realizes that she's arguing all by herself, is her "aha" moment. That's the moment she understands, "Uh oh, something changed, Mom isn't yelling back. I think I'd better be quiet now." It's at that moment when you use your Mommy-Daddy-firm-I'm-serious voice and say, "Are you done? I'm not going to talk until the yelling stops." Now all the power shifts back to you.

This is an extremely powerful remedy and will work for you for many years to come. Believe me, you'll want to begin this before the tween/teen years, when you'll really need it.

Quick View

- Do not engage in arguing. Remain silent until your child realizes she's arguing all by herself.
- Use your Mommy-Daddy-firm-I'm-serious voice and say, "Are you done? I'm not going to talk until the yelling stops."
- Ending a power struggle this way shifts all the power back to you.

61. "Freeze!" ~ It's Not Just a Game

When you see your child walking into danger, the last thing you need is for a power struggle to begin. That could actually cause her to ignore you and continue walking into the dangerous situation. Remember the game "Red Light/Green Light?" I loved playing it as a child. Did you know that some children's games are not just games? They have a teaching component to them too. "Red Light/Green Light", "Stop and Go", the "Freeze Game" and "Mother-May-I" are all games that teach listening, following instructions and self-control. It can save a child's life too. The "Freeze Game" saved my three-year-old from getting hit by a car!

Once a child has mastered these games, you can use them to teach other important lessons. My friend, Nicola Reiss Taggert, *The Executive Moms Coach*, used "Stop" and Go" signs on her daughter's door around age two, to help her remember when she needed to stay in bed and when she was allowed to get out of bed.

To use the "Freeze Game" to save a child from a dangerous situation, teach the game through play first. Then call a family meeting and tell the children that the word "Freeze," is no longer a "game" you play in your house. Tell them that if they ever hear Mom or Dad yell, "Freeze," they need to do just that—freeze. Tell them, "You freeze instantly and don't move because Mom or Dad sees something dangerous with their eyes that you haven't seen." You'll have about two to three seconds to act while they remain frozen. That two or three second bit of time was just enough time for me to grab my youngest and get him out of the path of an oncoming car.

Make sure to yell "Freeze" every now and then to make sure the kids really understand what to do. I always wanted to know how long saying something like, "Freeze" stays with a child. One Thanksgiving, as my nearly grown sons were doing the dishes, I yelled "FREEZE," and they froze where they stood. They looked at me and said, "What did we do?" I said, "Nothing. I just wanted to see if it still worked!" They shot me such a look, they didn't think it was funny!

Make sure to tell the kids they are never allowed to ignore the word "freeze" when it comes from a *trusted* adult.

Quick View

- Teach your children how to play the "Freeze Game." Once mastered, never use it as a game again.
- Tell them if they ever hear Mom or Dad yell "Freeze" they need to do just that—freeze.
- Tell them, "You freeze because Mom or Dad sees something dangerous with their eyes that you haven't seen."
- Yell, "Freeze," out of the blue every now and then to make sure the kids really understand the importance of responding to this word, and so you know that you can rely on it.

62. Questioning ~ Stopping a Power Struggle

Suppose it's time for bed, and you ask your child to clean up her toys. Her reaction is to stand there and scream "No!" *really* loudly. Do you scream "Stop it!" using a louder voice to show her who's in charge? Do you threaten to take away all her toys if she doesn't clean up now? If you do, you're caught in a reaction cycle. She reacted to you, then you reacted to her, and now she'll react back again, and so on.

Instead of getting trapped in a power struggle, look at the situation through the eyes of a child. Did you stop and ask her *why* she said "no" to you? Or did you just go into the mode of overpowering to show her you're the boss?

You may have better success if you calmly get down to her, level and look her in the eyes and say, "You sound mad. Why don't you want to clean up?" By asking her what's going on with her you may find out it's a simple little thing that can easily be resolved, so you can move on without a power struggle. She may want to dress her doll in pajamas so dolly is ready for bed. You may find that a developmental phase has occurred again and she's afraid to climb the stairs alone. Numerous things may be going on with her, but you'll never know unless you ask.

When you ask questions, you'll usually find that your child is happy to tell you what's going on, and cooperate with you because she felt heard. Also, it's so much easier this way.

Quick View

- Get down to your child's level and look her in the eyes and ask her why she isn't cooperating.
- If you don't ask, you'll never know if it's something that can be easily resolved, or needs further investigation.

CHAPTER

9

REACTING

63. Calm to Furious ~ Talk to Someone

If you go from calm to mad in 1.2 seconds every once in a while, that's normal. If you go from calm to furious in 1.2 seconds many times a day, you know you need to do something about it. The bigger problem is, since children copy what we do, they think it's normal to act that way, and may begin to act that way, too.

Figuring out why you become furious is a personal journey; no one can do it for you. Start by investigating where your anger is coming from. A good way to begin is to look at the other things in your life that are making you angry. See if any of the following questions rings a bell for you.

- Do you feel alone?
- Are you getting enough rest?
- Are you getting the support you want from your partner/spouse?
- Do you wish you were at home with your child, or wish that you were at work?
- Are you desperate for adult conversation?
- I'm sure you love your child, but do you like parenting?

That's just a random list to get the ball rolling. Try and find a therapist to talk to about this. You don't have to be in therapy forever; there are therapists who are willing to work on one issue with a client. Most therapists are accustomed to talking to people *before* booking a session so both parties can see if it's a good match. Use that time to see if the therapist is willing to work on just this one issue with you. If the therapist isn't willing to have a pre-booking call or isn't willing to work with you short term, then move on to someone who will.

Dealing with what's making you furious isn't fun, but keeping those feelings buried inside you is creating your anger. Addressing this will make you feel calmer, make your child feel safer, and help prevent your child from copying your behavior.

Quick View

- Going from calm to furious in 1.2 seconds sends the message to your child that this is way people are supposed to behave.
- Consider seeing a therapist to gain some tools to help you manage your quick rise to anger. You'll feel better, your child will feel safer, and won't copy your behavior.
- Find a therapist that's willing to work on one issue with you and go for it. Your emotional health is important to the emotional health of your child and family.

64. Don't. You. Dare. Say. That.

When children are disrespectful, mouth off, or use backchat, parents tend to blow a fuse. I was told as a child, "Children are to be seen and not heard." If I was disrespectful in any way, I was punished.

When I had kids, I did what all parents do; I began my parenting career by doing to my children what was done to me. I had no experience; I didn't know any better. I was speaking disrespectfully to them, but insisted they speak respectfully to me. It wasn't working. I knew that if I didn't change things now, when they were young, I wouldn't get any respect from them when they got older. The question was how to change it?

I began to think back to my childhood, and realized that being disrespectful was a lack of self-control on my part. Lack of self-control was understandable since I was young and still learning, but I was the one who chose to say something disrespectfully, especially when I knew I shouldn't.

After I had that "aha" moment, I knew our family needed a space where people could go to get back in control when they were emotional or disrespectful. This wasn't a place of punishment; it was just a place to chill out. If parent or child spoke to someone disrespectfully, the person who was disrespectful had to stop and get back under control, then try again. You can accomplish the same thing by creating a *chill out chair*. A chill out chair allows a child, or adult, to breathe, figure out a better way to express him or herself, and figure out how to apologize for being disrespectful.

Why not just use punishment to teach this lesson? All I can do is tell you about my experience. When my kids became a tween and a teen, the natural time when children pull away from parents and tend to be rude or disrespectful as a way to forge their independence, I was able to look at them and say, "I don't talk to you that way, so please don't talk to me like that. Please try again and begin with an apology. Use the chill out chair if you need to." And it worked! I suggest you start now, when your children are young, so this becomes a normal way of dealing with disrespect, mouthing off or backchat in your family. You'll be glad you did. (Backchat is a new term I'd never heard of. It means talking back.)

Quick View

- Create a chill out chair somewhere away from family activities or anything dangerous.
- A chill-out chair is a place to go and breathe, so you can decide a better way to express yourself, then try again.
- Begin now when your children are younger, so you can rely on this approach when they're tweens/teens.

65. "Hurry Up" ~ The Getting Dressed Game

Does your child make an ordeal out of getting dressed each morning because he knows getting dressed means he'll be saying good-bye to you soon? If so, then this *Getting Dressed Game* may really work for you.

Create a spinning wheel using a paper plate. Divide the plate into as many sections as needed to include all the pieces of clothing your child puts on each day. The game begins once he's in clean underwear. He gets to spin the wheel and whatever the spinner lands on is what he runs into his room to put on. He then comes back into your room, gets a kiss and gets to spin again. If it says sweater, and he hasn't put on a shirt yet, let him bring it to you, and have him "spin again."

What's nice about this little game is you get to keep track of his progress as he runs back and forth from your room to his room, plus he gets some special time with you. It's certainly a better way to begin the morning than yelling, "Will you hurry up and get dressed! We're going to be late, again!"

Quick View

- Create the *"Getting Dressed Game."*
- Make a spinning wheel using a paper plate.
- Divide the plate into as many sections as needed to include all the pieces of clothing your child puts on.
- Have him spin the wheel and whatever section the spinner lands on is what he runs into his room to put on.
- You get to keep track of his progress as he runs back and forth, and he gets some special time with you.

66. "Stop It!" ~ Does It Work?

Let me ask you a tough question. When you say, "Stop it," does your child stop, never to do it again? Or do you say, "Stop it," hoping that one day you'll say it, and she'll actually listen? I know when I said "Stop it" over and over again to my kids, I wondered if I sounded like the teacher in a *Peanuts* cartoon, "Mwa, mwa, mwa, mwa" and that's why they were ignoring me. If that's happening to you, consider changing the words you're using.

As adults, we're really good at telling our children what we *don't* want them to do. What we have forgotten to do is to tell them what we *want them to do instead* of what they're doing. Instead risking "stop it" from becoming background noise, try saying, "I need you to open your ears. What are you doing right now? Is that allowed? What should you be doing?" or "You're doing it; what should you be doing instead?" "You're doing it" is a shorthand version of "What are you doing," that is less accusatory.

Yes, you have to say a few more words, but it's worth it. Changing the words causes your child to listen because you're no longer using the words you usually use that she has learned to ignore. She has to think about what she's doing, and what she should be doing instead. The responsibility rests with her to "stop it."

When you use your words in this way, you're doing four things at once: you're stopping her behavior in its tracks; you're getting her full attention, because you've asked her a question; you're causing her to think about her behavior; and you're staying calm because she's doing all the work by thinking of the answers to your questions. Learning is occurring and that's magic for any parent!

Quick View

- Children learn to ignore "stop it" when they hear it all the time.
- Don't just tell your child what you *don't* want him to do. Tell him what you *want him to do instead* of what he's doing.
- Changing the words causes your child to listen, because you're no longer using words she has learned to ignore.

67. Taking Responsibility ~ 50/50 Rule

We all know it's better to use "I" messages instead of "you" messages, when an issue arises, so the other person doesn't feel blamed or attacked. Blaming or attacking can easily cause anyone to shut down and be unwilling to find solutions.

Beginning a conversation with "I" instead of "you" works really well with adults, but teaching it to children is difficult. This tip is my version for children. It teaches a child how to take responsibility and not blame others. I call it the 50-50 rule. It works with children around the age six or seven.

The rule states that when two people have a fight, one person is responsible for half of the feelings and reactions produced, and the other person is responsible for the other half. In other words, "It takes two to tango." It's simple to use, and is easier for kids to understand if you and hubby, the almighty adults, take 50% responsibility for a few situations in front of the kids first. Here's an example between parent and child, beginning with the original fight.

Mom: "You broke the window! You never listen; you just do whatever you want! You're grounded!"
Child: "You never let me do anything! All you do is tell me what to do. I hate you!"

After an exchange like that, parent and child could spin off into many arguments, abandoning the issue at hand.

Make sure to let everyone calm down before you begin. You'll probably need to help your child figure out his half of the situation in the beginning.

Here's what the 50-50 rule sounds like.

Mom: "I was wrong to scream at you. I was very angry. That's my 50%. What's your 50%?"

Child: " I was playing too close to the window and didn't listen when you told me to move."

Mom: "I don't like hearing, 'I hate you.' It hurts my feelings, because I love you, even when I'm mad."

Child: "I'm sorry. I didn't mean it."

Mom: "Thank you for saying that. You know we have to talk about how you're going to pay for this."

Child: "I have no money. I'm a kid!"

Mom: "Don't panic. Let's talk about how you can earn the money."

Since you're both calmer, you're able to remain focused on the event at hand and discuss how to resolve it. Almost certainly, a large number of chores will be involved in paying for the broken window, which is a great way to teach personal responsibility.

Quick View

- After an incident, let everyone's emotions calm down before discussing things.
- The parent begins by announcing the feelings and reactions she contributed, her 50%. Then the child says what his 50% was.

68. Think Before You Act ~ How to Begin

When a child misbehaves, and a parent isn't sure what to do, some parents begin lecturing until they're calm enough to decide what to do. We've all heard this advice: Give yourself a moment to think before you act; it will keep you calmer. The big question is what to do with your kids while you think? I don't know about your kids, but mine would press me to talk to them immediately so they could get it over with!

In order to take a moment so you can regain your ability to think, turn to your older child and say, "Stop—have a seat and please be silent. I need to think before I talk." For a little one say, "Sit on your bottom now and no talking. I need to think about my words." Have them sit at your feet or beside you on the sofa. If she begins to chatter, whine or cry to get you to deal with her now, offer a choice: "You can sit here and wait, or sit in timeout and wait. What do you want to do?"

This does several things at once. It stops any misbehavior in its tracks; it silently and firmly informs a child that a correction is coming; it communicates to your child that you're serious; and it gives you a moment or two to digest what's happened, so you can think of what to do next. This firm moment makes a big impression on children. It shows them you're in charge and teaches them that it's best to sit silently or things could get worse!

Quick View

- Create a moment to think before you act, to restore a sense of calm and stop things from escalating further.
- Have your child sit next to you and be silent while you think. It shows them how serious you are.
- If they begin to press you so they can get it over with, tell them a timeout is about to happen.

69. Warnings ~ Two Children, Two Types

How you give your child a warning really depends on your child's temperament. One child may need a warning that's direct and firm. Another child may need a warning that adds a bit more information. Only you can decide what your child needs.

We've all said, "I'm counting, and you don't want me to get to three!" And we all know what the next question is after that: "What *does* happen when I get to three? What *will* I do?" Since the parent isn't sure what he will do, most begin by saying, "I mean it. Listen to me or you're in trouble!" What the parent has actually done is show the child that nothing really happens when he reaches three, just the same old threats; no real action.

You'll have a much better chance of having any counting you do work if you say what *will* happen as you count. Your follow-through then becomes effortless because you've already announced what is going to happen. I'm not saying whether counting is or is not the right thing to do. I just know that many, many parents use counting, and I wanted to suggest they add a few things to their method to help make it work a little bit better.

A Strong-willed Child: A strong-willed child needs clear, firm directions and no wiggle room. It might sound like, "Please do not write in the book; that's 1." Wait five seconds and say, "I will come and take the book and the pen if you don't stop now; that's 2!" Wait five seconds and then say, "I see you chose not to listen; that's 3. I need the book and the pen right now." There's no wiggle room as long as you immediately enforce what you've said would happen.

A Sensitive Child: A sensitive child requires a softer voice, and maybe some eye contact. "Son, put my pen down. You're not allowed to use it to color; that's 1." Then wait ten seconds and repeat, "Son, put my pen down. You can use crayons or a pencil, but not my pen; that's 2." Then wait ten more seconds and announce, "That's 3. You chose not to put the pen down; I need to take the pen from you now." Then silently take the pen.

You can see that both warnings are basically the same; they're just adjusted to the natural temperament of the child. Both warnings have you enforce the decision your child has made to accept the consequence, instead of stopping what he was doing. This all happens in less than one minute, and is done calmly and firmly, at the same time. This teaches him that you mean what you say and you *will* take immediate action, without anger.

Quick View

- Use warnings that include telling a child what will happen if he doesn't cooperate.
- Slightly change your tone of voice to accommodate a strong-willed or a sensitive child.
- The amount of time you choose to wait before taking action is up to you, you know your child best.

70. When Annoyed ~ That's Your Moment

Most parents react to misbehavior after it's been fully played out, and then wait until they get home to do anything about it. The problem with that is, by the time they get home, their anger has increased dramatically, and their child's fear, anger or hysteria has also increased. Now the focus has switched from the misbehavior at hand, to dealing with the emotions the misbehavior and impending consequences are producing.

If you let your intuition guide you, you'll notice there's a moment that comes *before* your anger. There's a moment when you *first* become annoyed. That's the moment when you want to deal with things and make corrections—the moment of *first annoyance.*

There are several benefits to taking action at the moment your first annoyed. First, you're still calm enough to think. Second, you have the ability to see the situation clearly enough to decide whether you should get involved in order to change the direction things are going, or let the situation play out so the child can learn. No matter what you decide, you're calm enough to respond, which means being gentle and firm at the same time.

Being gentle and firm at the same time means you can walk up to your child and whisper in her ear versus yelling from across the room. It means you're able to enforce the rules she has forgotten by asking her questions instead of yelling "Stop it!" It also means you can calmly remove her from the situation, if necessary, which makes a huge impression on your child. Your calmness represents firmness to her, tells her you're in charge, and she can't talk you out of anything.

Acting when you first feel annoyed may or may not stop her reaction. Her reaction is simply her child-like way of expressing that she doesn't like this. Handling things when you're first annoyed is a wonderful habit to get into now, while she's still young. It will be invaluable as your children get older and situations become more complicated.

Quick View

- There is a moment that comes just after misbehavior and before you get angry. It's the moment when you first become annoyed.

- Consider making your correction when you first feel annoyed, so you can remain calm and thinking is possible.

- Doing this won't stop your child's reaction. Her reaction is her way of saying, "I don't like this."

CHAPTER
10

REAL LIFE

71. A Parent's True Job ~ Releasing

Other than loving your child, the true job of a parent is to teach that child how to manage his or her own life.

As parents, we all want our children to grow up to be successful adults. Sometimes in order to help a child grow, a parent needs to pull back and let the child experience the pain and consequences of his or her choices. No parent likes this. Every parent has the impulse to rescue his or her child from pain. All parents need to know that the impulse to rescue will always be there. It doesn't go away. You have to resist it and *choose* not to act on it. It can be one of the hardest things you do as a parent.

As adults, we can look back on our lives and see that our greatest teachings came from our biggest mistakes. If someone had taken that away from us, how much would we have learned? If you can remember this when the time comes to let your child learn from his or her choices, it will help you.

Candace Lienhart, a truly wise woman, once said to me, "Parenting is about slowly releasing a child to him or herself, bit by bit." I think that's the perfect way to sum up our jobs as parents.

Quick View

- For a child's personal and social growth, it is necessary to hold back the impulse to rescue your child from every pain or mistake that crosses her path.
- Children learn more from *their* mistakes than they do from your corrections.

72. Difficult Days ~ Teach Self-Reflection

We all have bad days. Young children have days that can be consumed by developmental challenges, unhappy parents and consequences.

Children have no real perspective on life. They don't really understand that things do change from one day to the next. They have no concept of the future because they live in the moment. They may wonder if they had a bad, unhappy day today, is everyday going to be that way from now on.

I used to make a point of telling my children, "You know what the best thing is about a bad day? It's over, and now you get to think about what you'll do differently tomorrow."

This helps a child learn that life changes from one day to the next, so, hopefully, they never feel boxed-in or desperate. This statement also begins teaching self-reflection long before development gives them that ability. They begin getting used to throughly looking at, and reviewing, their misbehavior so they can understand how to make sure it doesn't happen again. This is an invaluable asset for both parents and children to have as early as possible.

Quick View

* Let children know that tomorrow is a different day, and they can make it into anything they want.

73. Chores ~ Whirlwind Sunday

Every family is busy, and has chores that need to be done in order to keep the family moving along. When my kids were little my husband coined the phrase, "We all make the mess, so we all clean the mess, period!"

With that in mind our family created *Whirlwind Sunday*. Everyone started the day by being lazy. We would sleep a little later, and then I'd cook a big breakfast. Right after breakfast, we would all go in different directions to do our chores. We'd turn up the music and work in a fast and furious fashion so we could save part of the day for relaxation.

Each person was responsible for his or her room, part of a bathroom and one other chore. Hubby would do our bedroom and our bathroom, while I did the kitchen and dining room. Each child did his room and one part of his bathroom and they'd split the vacuuming. Hubby and I took turns dusting. It normally took an hour to an hour and a half to get the whole house clean.

If the children chose to be slowpokes, and they did try that a few times, they learned that their friends would just have to wait. They knew that this was the Sunday ritual in our family. Yes, they tried to negotiate their way out of it, but because it was the ritual, and had been since they were little, it was pretty easy to enforce.

Quick View

- Create a weekly cleaning ritual now so it's just the way things are in your family as your children grow.
- Make chores a family experience, instead of an individual, dreaded chore.
- Try not to insist that things must be perfect. Turn up the music and have some fun!

74. Family Dinners ~ Make Them Enjoyable

All the experts agree: family dinners need to happen so families can stay connected. In many homes, however, dinner is filled with arguing, and punishing that disrupts family time. However you can show children what you expect at the dinner table without yelling, punishing or interrupting dinner.

The first thing you need to do is accept that for a short time, maybe a few weeks, you won't be eating dinner with your child. Don't be alarmed; you'll get back to having family dinners every night. But right now, because family dinners are filled with yelling and chaos, you won't be eating together as you teach your child what you expect at the dinner table.

What you do is feed the children dinner first, and then invite them to join you for dessert. The key is you're inviting the children to join the adults for dessert *if* they can behave, follow the rules, and use their manners. Then, if you need to ask someone to leave the table while eating dessert, it doesn't compromise their healthy food intake; all they lose is dessert. And because dessert is a treat, children tend to learn how to behave rather quickly.

When the kids have proven that they understand the rules invite them to join you for dinner two or three times a week, for a week or so. Having them join you only a few times a week rather than nightly, makes dinner with the adults seem special. That's what causes them to be aware of the rules their behavior, and manners. Once they show you they can do well a few times a week, go back to having regular family meals.

Teaching your children how you expect them to act at the table not only encourages good behavior, but it also allows great conversations to take place, instead of yelling. Isn't that what family time is supposed to be about?

Quick View

- One way to teach children what you expect from them at the dinner table, begin feeding the children dinner first, separate from the adults.

- Invite the children to join you for dessert, only. That way if they misbehave, and have to leave the table, they're only sacrificing dessert, not losing dinner, which can cause them to whine and complain all night long.

- Have them join you once or twice a week for a family meal until they really get it. After that, return to daily family meals.

75. Punishment or Discipline ~ Which to Use?

Some parents think enforcing discipline and boundaries should be saved for the tween and teen years, and that younger children should simply be punished. They're shocked when I tell them that the *best* time to begin using discipline is during the first five years of life.

The first five years of life are when a child learns how daily life is handled, how to interact with others, and how to behave. This is when the brain is hard-wired. That's why it's more beneficial to a child if the corrections are presented through discipline instead of punishment. Discipline tends to be delivered with fewer intense emotions than punishment, and that, in and of itself, makes learning easier.

Here are some other differences between punishment and discipline that may help you decide what you want to do.

- Punishment makes a child feel as if she is paying for what she did. Discipline teaches a child what *not* to do, and what to do instead.

- Punishment makes someone else the authority in the situation. Discipline asks a child to think about why you've made this a boundary so they can learn for themselves.

- Punishment happens after a child has crossed the line, which can actually surprise a child. Discipline tells a child where the edge of the line is and what happens if they break the rules, so there are no surprises.

- Punishment usually stems from anger. Discipline causes self-reflection and teaches behaving this way doesn't work.

- Punishment causes a child to say what he or she thinks a parent wants to hear, so the punishment will stop. Discipline allows parent and child to ask each other questions so real understanding and learning can occur.

Which one do you think will teach more, empower a child more, and allow you to remain calmer?

Quick View

- The difference between punishment and discipline may not seem important to you now, but the way a child responds to each can make a world of difference to that child's future.
- Discipline really empowers a child to be responsible. Repeated punishment can create rebellion in later years.

76. Reconnecting ~ It's Over Now

Some parents feel as if they need to withhold attention or remain mad after they've enforced a boundary or corrected behavior. They believe that if they go back to being kind and supportive when things are complete, it might invalidate their authority, cause the child to think the misbehavior wasn't a big deal, or allow the child to repeat the behavior. As I said in tip #1, when a parent stops yelling while enforcing a firm boundary, what's revealed is just how firm the boundary really is. I believe that firmness is enough to make the point.

I think it's really important to go in and talk to your child when the consequence is over, so you can reconnect and show her that this is now resolved. Since your child is still reeling from the firmness you've just enforced, and the firmness did the teaching for you, you can have your talk using a kind and supportive tone, instead of one that sounds as if you're angry or lecturing.

Instead of being the big, bad parent, sit next to your child and perhaps even rub his or her back. If you think your child may lash out and hit or kick you, then just stand near him, but watch your body language. If your body is stiff and your arms are folded, then you're communicating that this isn't really over. But if you lean against the door in a relaxed manner with a softer expression on your face, your child will sense that things are coming to a close. If he says, "Go away," respect that, and try again in a little while. There's no need to reignite things and punish him for being disrespectful. He's still feeling the intensity of the firm boundary.

Making sure you and your child reconnect, after behavior has been corrected, is a great habit to get into. You'll want that habit firmly in place long before the tween and teen years begin.

Quick View

- Reconnecting is the last piece of the puzzle when you parent by responding instead of reacting.
- Although your firmness speaks for you, your child also needs to be *shown* the correction has come to an end.
- Have a chat as things are winding down, to express "I love you" and lets hug when you're ready. Don't punish your child further if he's still upset, lashes out or tells you to go away. He'll be ready to reconnect when he's ready. It's best not to force things.

77. Retrain ~ Athletes Can, So Can You

Have you ever noticed that as soon as you decide to change the way you're handling something, life sends you the perfect set of circumstances to see if you're actually going to follow through? I certainly have.

Just deciding to change isn't enough. The key to implementing change successfully is to make sure that you have a new plan, a new method, or, when it comes to parenting, that you have new words and skills to use, so you don't fall back into your old way of doing things when your child's behavior provokes you.

When an athlete realizes there's something she's doing that's no longer working, she immediately seeks out a coach to help her re-train. It's the same thing with parenting.

Parents need new methods and new words to use to help them "fake it until they make it," if you will. Coaching doesn't mean you're a bad parent; it's quite the opposite. The fact that you're willing to search for a different way of doing things makes you an excellent parent.

Quick View

- Once you've made a decision to change the way you do things, expect challenges to pop up to test you.
- Parenting is the biggest distance race you'll run. Be prepared for challenging situations by being proactive. Figure out ahead of time what you will do. Use a coach, if need be, to help you create a good parenting plan.
- If you are enjoying the techniques in this book and would like more support, contact me for a coaching session at: www.proactiveparenting.net

78. Sex ~ And the Big Question

Parents often ask me what they should say when a child asks, "Where do babies come from?" Instead of panicking, throw the question back in your child's lap: "Where do you think babies come from?" The way your child answers will tell you the level of knowledge he or she has on the subject, and where you should begin.

Warning: One question does *not* mean it's time to give her *all* the details. Be brief and answer only the question your child has asked. If she has more questions, she'll ask them.

You have plenty of time in life for the "big talk." When my kids were tweens, I wondered if I'd ever had the big sit-down-sex-talk with them. I couldn't remember, so I asked them. They said, "Yes and no." I was confused. They said, "We did have a big talk once, but sex, bodies, love and babies have always been part of our normal conversation."

I believe that casually talking about sex and babies teaches children that it's a natural part of life, which it is. Talk openly and age-appropriately when you see scientific information about the human body. Make a comment or two when you see a respectful, loving relationship on TV or in movies. This reinforces the values you're trying to teach your children. When you're both ready, have the big sit-down-talk just to make sure you've filled in all the details.

Quick View

- Don't be afraid of a question about where babies come from.
- Always give out age-appropriate information.
- Simply answer what you were asked, and let it drop until she brings it up again. Trust me, she will.

79. Snacks ~ Can Be *Real* Meals, Too!

There's always a "push-and-pull" at dinnertime. The kids are starving and want a snack, and parents want them to save their appetites for dinner.

What if you served part of dinner as a snack? Yes, it uses a portion of the meal you were planning to eat as a family, but it solves the "hungry *now*" issue. Or you could allow the kids to have two or three carrot sticks, peanut butter or tuna on celery, or hummus or eggplant spread and crackers. Any of those choices are better than serving chips or having your kids become ravenously hungry and cranky.

You can make it "special" by letting them make the snack and eat it from a special plate. Not only is it food you have approved, you're also able to finish cooking dinner. If they get full from the snack they made, it's not such a big deal. At least they ate a healthy portion of their dinner!

Quick View

- Instead of making the kids save their appetite for dinner consider using part of dinner as a snack.
- Let the children eat their veggies, present it as a snack. Remember you can offer healthy dipping sauces, too.
- If you have trouble getting kids to eat heathy foods, try tip #34.

80. The Family Story ~ A New Ritual

Family gatherings have long provided entertainment, pre-served traditions, stories and memories of those who came before us. To keep those memories alive for your children and grandchildren try creating a new holiday ritual that blends the old with the new.

Instead of the annual family newsletter, ask each person, especially older ones, to think of five short stories to share with the family: One about raising their kids; one from their childhood; one about their parents, maybe including a family tradition they had when they were small; and one about their grandparents, and a current story.

Consider recording or video taping this, especially for the older members of your family. The wonderful benefit to recording a beloved family member is you, and future gen-erations, will get to see and hear them each time you listen to the cherished family stories. Doing this preserves your precious family's history, and believe me, your children will thank you.

Here are two websites to get things rolling:
http://oralhistory.library.ucla.edu/familyHistory.html
http://genealogy.about.com/cs/oralhistory/a/interview.htm

Quick View

- Instead of the traditional "what we did this year" newsletter, have each member of the family write or record five short stories to share.
- The stories can focus on raising kids, childhood memories, parents and/or grandparents, a current life event or family traditions.
- Nominate a different person each year to be the historian so one person isn't always stuck with the job.

81. What a Mess! ~ What Should You Do?

Getting children to clean up a spill or mess can turn into a power struggle. One way to avoid that is to let the kids clean up their own messes by following a list of questions that cause thinking. You know that it may not be done as well as if you did it, but time and practice will take care of that!

Post a series of questions on the refrigerator to cause a child to think about the process of cleaning up. An older child can answer the questions and do most of the cleanup on his own, while you observe. Take pictures so a younger child can figure out the clean-up process too, just like they do in school.

Some of the questions you might want to begin with are.
- "What messes are you *not* allowed to clean up?
- "Is this a wet mess or a dry mess?"
- "What tools do you need for wet/dry messes?"
- "Where does the mess end up, in the sink or the garbage?"
- "What will this mess look like when it's cleaned up?"
- "Will you be using my version of 'clean' or yours?"
- "What happens if this is not done as we agreed?"
- "What should you do first, second etc.?"
- "Where do you put things when you're all done with them?"

Those questions naturally point out all the rules and expectations you have for cleaning up. It also means you don't need to be the clean-up police or, resentfully do it yourself.

Quick View

- Put the general steps for cleaning up messes on a list.
- For those children who don't read, take pictures of your child cleaning up a mess so she knows what to do.
- Children really are capable of cleaning up a mess. It teaches them: "You make a mess, you clean a mess!"

CHAPTER

11

RULES

82. Rules ~ A Picture Is Worth...

All children need to know their family's rules, even if they're semi-verbal or can't read yet. One good solution for semi-verbal non-readers is to use pictures. A perfect example is hitting a sibling. Take two pictures, one in which your child is playing nicely as she plays with her sister, and one picture showing her hitting her sister. Make a sign using both pictures and write the rules under the pictures.

Instead of yelling when she hits her sister, walk your child to the sign and ask, "Which picture is a "no" in our family?" Then ask, "Which picture shows how we play?" Then have her go apologize or do a "makeup" as described in tip #25. This way of handling the rules stops parents from having to announce the rules repeatedly, and yell and punish.

Creating pictures and asking your child questions about those pictures gives her all the information she needs to learn, and tells her how resolve the situation at the same time. This works so well it's used in many, many classrooms with great success.

Quick View

- Take a picture of your child following the rules and one where she isn't following the rules.
- Using photos and words allows all ages to answer the question, "Do we act like this in our house?"
- Pictures help a parent respond by eliminating the need constantly repeat the rules.

83. School Rules ~ Practicing at Home

Some children have a harder time than others adjusting to school rules. They struggle with sitting in circle time or they talk at their desks or they ignore the class rules and so on.

The first thing to do is ask the teacher if she thinks your child really knows the rules, and why she thinks he's having a problem remembering them? If it's something you can handle without a professional, try focusing on the issue by practicing at home.

Younger Children: Suppose your child is having difficulty sitting still during circle time. Get some blue painter's tape and make a large circle in the living room to replicate circle time at school. (Read the directions to make sure the tape won't ruin your carpet.) Each day for one week, read stories while he practices how to sit at circle time. You can make up little tricks, like having him tuck his hands under his legs to help him sit still.

Older Children: Suppose your child talks in class when he's supposed to be working silently. Use homework time as an opportunity to teach him how to do no talking and fidgeting (notice the age appropriate words) by setting-up a pretend classroom at your kitchen table. Your other children aren't allowed to disturb the two of you during this time.

Your child sits and does his homework while you read. Simply mark down how many times he wiggles or begins to talk. When his homework is done, show him the list you've made. The idea is to teach him to "better his best" each day so he can get to the point where he follows the rules automatically. The point is not to punish, as it will slow-down your child's learning process.

Discuss tricks to stay silent. He can silently hum a song in his head instead of talking out loud. Teach him how to focus on one part of his homework or work sheet at a time. Try placing a blank sheet of paper over the bulk of the work-sheet and let him move it as needed so he isn't overwhelmed by what's left to do.

Once a child has proven to himself that he can accomplished sitting still or working silently at home, he'll feel more capable of doing it at school. It's the repetition of doing it every day, over the course of a week or so, that drives the learning. Many parents feel that it's a teachers job to give this type of instruction. A teacher has too many students and too much to do to offer one-on-one help like this to each student who needs it.

Quick View

- Set up a pretend-classroom at home.
- Each day, for a week or so, practice *how* to do whatever your child is having trouble with.
- The repetition of practicing these new skills every day, over the course of a week, is what drives the learning.

84. Bribe or Reward ~ Very Different

When a parent is tired or frustrated, he'll do almost anything to make a child do as asked. The problem with bribing is a bribe puts a child in control of the situation. When you reward, however, the parent remains in control of the situation. Let me explain.

- A *bribe* is offered *before* a child does something she was asked to do. The child gets to decide if the bribe is good enough to do something she doesn't want to do.

- *Rewards* are not mentioned until *after* a child does something she was asked to do. The parent gets to decide if the child did the job in a way that deserves a reward or not. The parent has the control because nothing has been announced yet.

- *Bribes* beget bribes, and usually need to increase in frequency and size in order to be effective. *Rewards* allow a parent to decide how often to give them so they aren't expected each time.

- A child can reject a *bribe* if she doesn't want to do the task, leaving the parent no choice but to up the ante in order to gain cooperation. A child cannot influence a *reward,* except by doing a good job, which was the parent's ultimate goal in the first place.

- *Bribes* tend to become an expected part of the deal, and are usually demanded with an entitled tone of voice. *Rewards* are seen as a way to say "Thanks," so they remain special and memorable.

Which one do you want to use?

Note: This tip does not apply to the use of rewards as a behavior modification tool. Behavior modification is used for many things, and addresses completely different situations than those discussed in this book.

Quick View

- On the surface, bribery seems like a good way to make a child do as asked, but bribes can get out of hand quickly.
- Rewards are a way parents can say, "Thank you," and help the parent avoid all the negative side effects of bribery.

85. "But, I forgot" ~ Not an Excuse

Children really believe that saying, "I forgot," after they've broken a rule, is enough to get them out of trouble, and can get pretty upset when those words don't work. Parents, on the other hand, believe that forgetting is part of the problem. Some parents will even add more punishment or another consequence for forgetting.

Children need to experience something from start to finish in order to learn all about it. Your child needs to be able to say "I forgot" so she can learn it's not a good defense strategy. She needs to experience that consequences still happen, even if you say, "I forgot."

Being punished for saying "I forgot" has a different outcome than you think. Punishment doesn't teach her not to say "I forgot." It simply makes her think that her parents are mean and just won't listen. She then increases the drama, crying, and pleading to *get* them to listen. Now the conversation remains stuck on the "but I forgot" part of the situation and seldom comes back around to the fact that the child broke the rules in the first place.

If, on the other hand, you post your family's rules, or use pictures for pre-verbal children (see tip #82) where your child can clearly see them, you can walk him up to the posted list of rules and say, "Which rule did you break? And what happens when you break that rule?" Doing that allows your child to see that the "I forgot" defense has no influence over the situation. When you break a rule, the consequence follows anyway, especially since it's been posted on the refrigerator, right where everyone can see it.

Skipping over the "I forgot" defense and correcting the situation anyway, stops you from reacting. Just walk over to where the rules are posted and point. Right about that time your child realizes that "I forgot" isn't going to work.

Quick View

- Punishing a child for saying, "I forgot" only makes her think you're not listening, which causes her to beg and cry louder.
- Pointing to the rules you have posted helps reduce the possibility of a reaction and tells her all she needs to know.
- Proceed with the consequence for the original issue and say, "Will saying 'I forgot' change my mind?"

86. Junk Food or Healthy ~ Pig (out) Day

My kids, like all kids, begged for the "unhealthy" food they saw in the grocery store or on TV. I'd say "No" over and over again, and they'd whine and complain over and over again. Then I began to notice how often they were asking to go to a friend's house for lunch or dinner, and coming home hyped-up on sugar. I realized they were eating candy and chips and drinking soda at the neighbor's house. That's when I remembered a funny name that friends of mine gave to a day when they ate whatever they wanted. They called it *Pig Day*.

In our house we instituted *Pig Day* on Saturdays. We allowed our kids, if they ate reasonably well during the week, to eat whatever they wanted on Saturday. The first thing they learned was moderation. They got a chance to feel what it was like to have a belly full of junk food, and the resulting nausea from it. Soon, instead of fighting about food all the time, I was able to replace my constant "No" with "Yes, you can have it. Will you be eating it for breakfast, lunch or dinner on *Pig Day?*"

Quick View

- *Pig Day* is a day when children can eat whatever they want.
- Allowing children to eat what they want one day a week changes the constant "No" to "Yes you can have it. Will you be eating it for breakfast, lunch or dinner on *Pig Day?*"
- *Pig Day* is a great way to teach moderation and allows a child to gain first hand experience with the types of food that can give you a stomach ache.

CHAPTER

12

SELF-ESTEEM

87. I'm Proud of You ~ 25 Times a Day?

We've all witnessed children who constantly ask, "Did you see me?" after they've done an ordinary task. It's an unconscious request for praise. This habit begins due to what a child assumes is normal. When a parent constantly says, "Good job" after every little thing a child does, the child thinks that's normal and expects external validation and acknowledgement after everything they do.

There are three problems with external validation.

Problem #1: As stated in tip #88, if you say "good job" all day, every day, at some point your enthusiasm and sincerity will fade. If that happens, your child may gravitate toward misbehavior to get a blast of attention and approval. See tip #17.

Problem #2: The real world is not in the habit of validating everything we do. If a child has been raised to see their self worth through the eyes of others, they will most certainly feel let down by the outside world.

Problem #3: When others have been in charge of determining a child's self worth, a child becomes far more susceptible to peer influence and bullying.

Your child won't always be in your presence, they'll need to know, without a shadow of a doubt, that they are worthy in order to withstand outside influences and opinions. The following tips will share ways for your child to discover, and maintain, true high *self*-esteem.

Quick View

- The key to how to build high self-esteem is to focus on the word "self." Parents need to help kids find ways to discover their own true worth, instead of relying on external validation.

88. Compliment or Notice ~ Fill Her Up

When you ask parents what their number one goal for their child is, they often answer, "To make sure my child has high self-esteem." The norm these days is to praise and applaud your child in as many ways and as many times as possible, every day. See tip #89 and #90 for more on that. The problem is, after a while, the praise and applause can begin to feel hollow to both parent and child.

We all know people who relentlessly compliment others. When you first get a compliment from them you appreciate it. Then, after a while, you begin to see that they say nice things about everyone for everything, and the praise begins to feel insincere. The same thing can happen between parent and child.

One smart way to avoid that from happening is to simply *notice* instead of compliment. When your child does something, instead of using an excited voice to praise how wonderful she is, try saying, "I noticed that you did your homework with no fuss today. Thanks." When you simply notice something your child has done, she gets the opportunity to applaud herself, versus you having to be the one who always does it. Having her congratulate herself is the true definition of "self" esteem—feeling good about your *self*, no matter what!

Quick View

- Saying "I *noticed*" is a great way to remedy the problem of praising and applauding everything all day long.
- When you "notice" something, it causes a child to look at what you noticed and applaud herself.
- Self-applause is a key factor in "self" esteem, since self-esteem is feeling good about your *self*, no matter what!

89. Self Assessment ~ Better Than Praise

Everyone knows a person who does things, or helps someone, in order to get noticed. No one intends to raise a child who's a people-pleaser. So, how can you avoid it? It *is* important to praise and applaud your child.

Instead of always saying "I'm proud of you," flip it around and say, "You must be proud of yourself," or "You can be proud; that's a job well done." When you switch from "I'm proud," to "You must be proud," you're teaching your child to look at his own work and applaud himself. You're also showing him that there's a feeling of pride that occurs inside of you when you do a good job, and that's a feeling worth striving for. An added benefit is he won't grow up to be a people-pleaser, constantly seeking others to compliment him regularly.

Make sure that you read tip #90 so you understand that *how* you praise is more important than the praise itself. This tip shows you how to teach your child to applaud himself.

Quick View

- Instead of always saying, "I'm proud of you," flip it around and say, "You must be proud; that's a job well done."
- Switching from "I'm proud" to "You can be proud; that was a hard day of work" teaches a child it's okay to look at his own work and applaud himself.

90. Two Types of Praise ~ One Can Backfire

Praise is a wonderful way to express "I love you." However, when a parent praises *everything* a child does, the effect can actually diminish self-esteem.

Ask Moxie.com had this to say about self-esteem, after reading *NurtureShock* by Po Bronson and Ashley Merryman. "Bronson and Merryman looked at research by Carol Dweck showing that kids who were praised for intelligence ended up giving up in the face of challenge, while kids who were praised for effort were more persistent when challenged. ...when they were told they were smart, that made them self-conscious and afraid of proving that they weren't smart, so they wouldn't try things they weren't good at."

Did you know that there are two kinds of praise? One is called "global" and the other is "specific." Global praise sounds like, "You're great," or "You're the best at math." This type of praise doesn't share any details a child could use to repeat the success. And it's structured in a way that might be misinterpreted by a child to mean, "I'm better than my peers."

Specific praise sounds like, "I saw how much effort you put into re-working that sentence to include spelling words, you should be proud." Or "It takes a long time to sort through the blocks to find and use only red ones, nice job."

Specific praise applauds the effort used. It inspires persistence because the details needed to repeat the success are included. Specific praise works to build self-esteem because there's little room to doubt its sincerity. There's too much detail involved for it not to be true.

A great way to remind yourself to use specific praise is to begin sentences with, "I noticed..." or "I saw how..." or "Looks to me like you..." Beginning sentences that way automatically forces you to insert specific details, i.e. specific praise.

Parents also have a tendency to add "good girl" or "good boy" to the end of a sentence. But saying that can backfire as well. Saying "good girl" or "good boy" can create a self-sacrificing adult always looking for acknowledgement of what they've done. Instead of unconsciously adding "good girl" or "good boy" to the end of a sentence, simply add a "Thank you," when appropriate.

Quick View

- Try and remember to add details to the praise you offer so it informs a child of what's needed in order to repeat their success.
- To remind yourself to use specific praise begin sentences with statements like, "I noticed you..." or "I saw how you..." or "Looks to me like you..."

91. "It's Too Hard!" ~ Rising to the Occasion

When a child says, "This is too hard!" parents want to stop the whining and complaining immediately, because they know a long rant has begun that will probably end in a power struggle. Some parents just say, "It's not too hard. Stop whining!"

One way to stop the whining and complaining, and to get the job done, is acknowledge the child's feelings. The moment the complaining begins is *not* the moment to allow him to quit the task. If you do, he's learned that when things get too hard, it's okay to give-up. And no parent wants to teach that!

If you acknowledge his feelings and add a dose of encouragement, he'll still hem and haw a bit, but you'll be amazed at what happens. Try saying, "Yes, this is hard, and I know you can do it."

Your child whines or complains because experience has taught him that, when he does he's sent to timeout, and when timeout is over, he gets to go play, because Dad has decided it would be easier to just do the chore himself. Swooping in and doing it yourself, instead of your child, doesn't teach him how to push past the hard part and keep going.

Each time he whines, instead of reacting to him, repeat, "I know this is hard and I know you can do it." Soon he'll see there's no getting out of doing the task and he'll shift from complaining to showing you how hard he's working. He's reacting to having his feelings acknowledged instead of condemned. He's rising to the occasion because you have faith that he *can* do this. Now he really does deserve to hear, "You can be proud of yourself. That is a job well done!"

Quick View

- Acknowledging that a job is hard tells a child that he's been heard.
- Having faith in his *ability* to do the job inspires him to show you just how hard he *can* work.
- When the work is done, use what you have learned about praise in this book and say, "You can be proud of yourself. That is a job well done!"

CHAPTER

13

SEPARATION ANXIETY

92. Crying: Part 1 ~ The School

When it comes to going to school, some children have a hard time separating from a parent. They can't seem to walk into school without a fuss, a meltdown or a full-blown tantrum. The teacher usually says, "Give them time. They'll be okay." And most children do settle down once they're engaged in the fun or interesting school activities.

For some, however, just getting them to let go can be a heart-wrenching scene every morning. Before you attempt part two of this tip, consider if any of the following may be happening to you or your child. If either point strikes a chord with you, then part two of this tip is *not* for you at this time.

1. If deep inside yourself you're conflicted or really sad to see your child head off to school, then you need to know that your child can feel that, even if you don't say a word about how you feel. All your child knows is you're a tense Mom at school and a relaxed Mom at home, and she doesn't understand why.

She's young and may decide if Mom is uneasy, then this may not be a safe place, and will cry or cling to you. You then misinterpret why she's crying and decide that she isn't ready to go to school. This circle of behavior will continue until *you are* really ready to let go and send her off to school.

The second part of this tip depends on your being really ready to send her to school or it will backfire. That's why if you resonate with what you just read, then part two of this tip is *not* for you at this time.

2. The other reason not to move on to step two is if your intuitive sense is telling you that this isn't the best environment for your child. Always follow your instincts in situations like this. Don't ignore it; it's a message you don't want to miss.

Quick View

If you don't resonate with either of these two points, then, if you like, move on to part two.

- It's possible that the unexpressed hesitancy a parent feels, as she's leaving her child at school, tells her child that she's uncomfortable dropping her off. That fear can cause a child to cry and cling to a parent. The parent then misinterprets the crying and clinging as an indication the child isn't ready for school. This circle of behavior will continue until *the parent* is really ready to send her off to school.
- When a parent is *really* ready to send her child to school, she can use part two of this tip to help her.

93. Crying: Part 2 ~ The Method

If your intuition is telling you that *now* is the time to help your child learn to separate from you, so she can go into school without crying or clinging to you, then this tip *may* help. You'll need to be strong and committed to doing this, because even this method doesn't change things overnight.

What you're going to do is create confidence through consistency, by using the same words and actions each day. Using this method creates a touchstone of confidence for your child, as she discovers her inner strength to let go.

The concept is simple, but emotionally challenging to apply.

- You'll need the same teacher to meet you at the entrance to the school each morning.
- You'll be using the same words and using the same actions every single day. Tell your child, "I have to go and I'll be back at noon," or whenever you normally pick her up. Telling your child the time you'll be back allows the teacher to have her look at the clock when she misses you, and figure out how many more hours or minutes it will be before you arrive.
- Tell her "I love you," give her a kiss and hand her to the teacher.
- She *will* cry and use her body to reach out for you. You'll *need* to turn around and walk to the car.

Most parents think, "If I stay a little longer, she'll be more able to handle the separation." There are two problems with this. First, you've probably already stayed longer to comfort her and it hasn't worked. The other problem is what your face and body look and feel like to your child as you're trying to comfort her.

Despite the fact that you're trying to calm her down, you're still anxious about the scene you see unfolding; therefore, your face and body are tense. Your child senses your tension and decides, Mom is as upset as I am. I hope you can see that staying longer to comfort your child tends to keep the circle of upsetting behavior going between the two of you.

However, when you turn around and walk away, you're sending a silent message of confidence backed up by a real-world experience.

What do I mean by "backed-up by a real-world experiment?" Your child sees and feels your confidence as you walk away. This shows her she can rely on your confidence. She thinks, If you feel confident about leaving me here, then I'll trust you." Your real world confidence allows her to summon up her courage and face the day. Returning exactly at the agreed-upon time, and not being late, reaffirms that she can trust you and your words.

It takes several days, or more, to do this. If you and the teacher don't see signs of change within two weeks, then it's time to look for other possible causes of the separation anxiety.

I'll be honest; a crying child is really hard to walk away from. You can go cry in the car if you need to—I know I did.

Quick View

- Make arrangements to have the same teacher meet you and your child at the entrance of the school each day for two weeks.
- Use the same words and actions every day to inspire trust and confidence.
- Be strong until you reach your car. You can let your feelings out in the car after you pull away, if you need to.

94. Crying: Part 3 ~ The Sadness

Once you've left your child at school, you'll probably begin wondering how she's doing. You'll wonder if she's crying or if she's having fun. There is a way to find out, and help your child feel heard all at the same time.

No matter how old your child is get her a personal journal and put it in her cubby, or some place where she can easily get to it. If she can write, give her a pen. If she can't write, give her a sheet of happy ☺ and ☹ sad stickers. Tell her each time she feels happy or sad during the day she can go to her cubby and write the word that best describes how she's feeling, or put a ☺ or ☹ sticker in the journal. When you review the journal each day and combine that information with what the teacher tells you, and you'll get a pretty accurate idea of how your child is doing.

The journal also lets your child know that she's being heard and not just being dropped off at school. As you're gather her belongings at the end of the day, take time to look at the journal together. If she had a ☺ day, congratulate her.

If she had a ☹ day, let her know it's okay; it happens to everyone, once and a while. Assure her that tomorrow is another day, one that could be easier. She *will* use your faith in her when she needs it the most, when you're not there and she's confronted with missing you.

When she's had a ☺ day, refrain from any additional rewards. Let the fact that it was a happy day be the reward. If you take her for ice cream on a happy day, it sends the message, "I was good today so I get a treat, but when I had a sad day I don't get a treat." That type of thinking could backfire. Your child may decide to always tell you his day was happy, even when it wasn't, in order to get the treat. It can also lead to misunderstandings about expressing feelings in the future.

Quick View

- A journal allows a child to deposit her feelings somewhere, so she feels heard, and can go back to join the class.
- Look at the journal with her each day and encourage her if needed. If it was a sad day, ask her if there was anything in particular that made it sad. If not, let her know being sad at school is okay, now and then, and tomorrow is another day.
- Refrain from giving rewards on good days, and withholding rewards on sad days.

95. Crying: Part 4 ~ The Sitter

This is the same basic idea as leaving your child at school, but with a few additions, because this is done at home. Here again, you're creating a touchstone of confidence backed up by a real-world experience. It's CRUCIAL, for the success of this tip, that you be true to your word and return exactly when you say you're going to return.

- Hire one sitter to come every day for one to two weeks. Choose a sitter who's fun, reliable, and will be available for one month in order to successfully teach your child about the babysitting experience.
- Tell the sitter she'll be at your house for five minutes the first day, 15 minutes the second day, 30 minutes the third and so on for one to two weeks, depending on how long it takes the child to feel comfortable with having a sitter.
- Tell your child, "Suzie is going to stay with you while Mommy goes out for five minutes. What's crucial here is that you don't run an errand which might prevent you from getting back in five minutes. Just get in your car and drive down the street so your child can't see you.
- Tell the sitter that if your child cries, that's okay. The sitter is to stand by the clock and let the child see how fast five minutes is ticks by.
- Extend the time you're away each day, until your child is no longer fazed by the fact that you're leaving.
- Have the same sitter come babysit once or twice a week for a couple of hours so your child can get comfortable with someone watching him while you are out.

This really works, and usually takes less time than you'd think. Remember, you're not harming your child emotionally; you're helping him move past his fears.

Quick View

- Hire one sitter to help you teach this, who will be available to when you need her for about a month. That way, your child doesn't have to adjust to a new sitter as he's learning to let you go out.

- Always be home, when you say you will be home so your child begins to trust that you will return.

CHAPTER
14

SIBLINGS

96. Siblings ~ "You Love Him More!"

If you suspect one of your children thinks you love his sibling more than you love him, here's a tip that uses a picture of a heart to help you bring the subject up. Make sure the picture isn't graphic in any way; you can even draw one yourself.

Sit your child down and ask him, "Do you think I love your brother more than you?" Then say nothing and wait for him to speak up to tell you how he sees it. Don't try to talk him out of how he sees things because he'll never believe you, he needs to have his own "aha" moment. If he doesn't answer you, move on.

Tell him, "Here's a picture that shows you that it's impossible for me to love one of you more than the other. You know that love lives inside of your heart, right? Take a look at the picture of the heart. You can see it has four special places where love lives—the four chambers. Each special place in the heart has enough love in there for a lifetime and there are enough special places in my heart for everyone in our family. So, the next time you feel like I love your brother more than I love you, come and ask for a heart hug (a bear hug) so you can remember my heart has plenty of love in it for all of my children."

Quick View

- Never underestimate the power of a photo or a drawing to illustrate your message.
- If you have more than four children in your family, divide the chambers so there is a chamber space available for every person in the family.

97. Fighting Siblings ~ Assumptions

When siblings fight, parents may become so infuriated that they charge in, assume who's right and who's wrong, and then decide how things will be resolved. The truth is a parent's assumption may not always be correct. There are times when one child provokes the other child, but all the parent hears is the provoked child's reaction and resulting fall-out.

The only way to avoid these situations is to install cameras in all the rooms so you can review the video. Since that's not going to happen, it might be wise for parents to remain neutral and help guide the siblings toward resolution, avoiding assumptions and favoritism.

Here are two examples:

Mom: "Who screamed and why?"
Becky: "Mom, Maggie won't let me use the play-dough!"
Mom: "Who do you need to work this out with, me or Maggie?"
Becky: "With Maggie, but she won't listen!"
Mom: "How do you think you should say it so she hears you? With mean words or nice words?"
Becky: "With nice words, but what if she won't share?"
Mom: "I'll be standing right beside you, helping both of you, if you guys can't work it out."
Mom: "Maggie, why won't you let Becky use the play-dough?"
Maggie: "Because I was using it first! Becky just wants to play with it because I am."
Becky: "That's not true. I want to play with it because I want to play with it, not because she's playing with it!"
Mom: "Here are two suggestions. You girls decide which one to use. I will hold the play-dough until you can agree on what will happen. Or you can set the timer and each person takes a turn. What would you like to do?"

Here's another conversation heard in many homes where there are siblings.

Mom: "What did you do to your brother?"
Child: "Nothing."
Mom: "Then why is he crying?"
Child: "I don't know."
Mom: "What do you mean you don't know?" (Things tend to go downhill from here.)

What if the conversation sounded like this instead?

Mom: "What do you think your brother's crying is trying to tell us?"
Child: "That he wants his toy back."
Mom: "That's good. You know him really well. What do you think you should do now?"
Child: "Give it back."
Mom: "Do you think a kiss and saying 'I'm sorry' would be good, too?"
Child: "Okay."

In both of these situations, the parent isn't deciding who is right or wrong. She's just helping the children figure out a better way to respond to each other. When parents handle basic, everyday fights this way both children learn how to communicate, they get the support they need, and the sibling relationship is preserved. Parents need to let their children know that the sibling relationship needs tender loving care because it's the one relationship that outlasts parents.

Quick View

- Handling the sibling conflict the way the tip recommends goes a long way towards creating lifelong closeness between siblings.
- Parents need to remind siblings, as they grow, to be kind to each other because the sibling relationship outlasts parents.

98. Rivalry & Siblings ~ Best Book Ever

If you haven't read *Siblings Without Rivalry* by Mazlish and Faber, then put this book down and go get it immediately. I'd recommend you get it from the library first, to make sure it's a good fit for you. Then buy it, because you'll want to keep it, write in it and paper clip the situations you encounter every day!

Of all the books I've read on siblings and rivalry, and I've read a lot, I believe *Siblings Without Rivalry* tells the honest truth about what siblings fight over, what it sounds like when a parent gets in the middle between siblings, and what parents can say and do so they can respond. It's the best book on the subject I've found!

Quick View

- I think that about says it. I loved this book. It transformed my role as a mother. It's that good.

99. Sharing ~ Older Children

No parent likes to hear siblings fight over a toy. Most parents either yell, "Stop it or you're both getting a time-out," or "Share it right now, or else!" as if those were magical phrases that would solve the problem instantly.

The problem with those two statements is the parent has only demanded that the children stop and share. No one has taught the children *how* to negotiate sharing. If you teach your children how to negotiate sharing, they'll be able to use those skills as they get older, when sharing becomes more complicated. So, how do you teach children to negotiate sharing?

You begin by calmly walking in and silently extending your hand. This gesture tells the children to put the object that's being fought over into your hands. Tell them the object will be waiting for them while they work this out. Then become a neutral facilitator and ask a series of the same questions to both children. Begin with one child, then turn to the other child and ask the exact same questions. *Ex: Notice the 3rd and 4th question below. The same question is asked to each child.*

Here's an example.

Mom: "What do you have to say about this?
         What do you want to happen?
         Can you give him what he wants?
         Can you give your sister what she wants?
         What ideas do you have to make this happen?
         Do you like any of those ideas?"

If you hit a stalemate, see if this opens things up.

Mom: "Well, I see no one is willing to share, and no one has any ideas, so I will keep this object until you guys figure out what to do."

This process requires that the children figure out what *they* want, and how to get it without harming or being rude to a person they love. This process prepares children for future friendships, for wife/husband or partner relationships, and for representing himself, or herself, in business.

Quick View

- Sharing is not only necessary during childhood; it's also a skill adults use in relationships.
- When you ask the same question to both children, they see they are equal, and learn how to say what is true for them and not buckle under to anyone else.

100. Sharing ~ Young Children

Most children go through a period of time when they have issues with sharing. This next tip is a good one that I learned years ago. I'd give credit to the brilliant person who created it, but I can't remember who did!

Sharing is never something that's easily accepted. Young children tend to see their toys as extensions of themselves. So when we ask them to share, from a child's perspective, it's as if we're asking them to give their right arm away for a little while, even though we promise to give it back. It's no wonder they vehemently say, "NO!"

Here, again, changing the words may help ease the situation. Try asking young children, "Will you need one or two minutes before you're ready to share?" Of course most children will choose two minutes because it is the bigger number. That question tells her that sharing *will* be happening and empowers her by allowing her to make the choice between one minute and two minutes.

The key is what *you* do while she's playing with the disputed object. You play with the waiting sibling or friend. Young children will usually drop the object and come over to join the fun, and the drama is over. Older kids will hold onto it until the last second before giving it up. This is just a little re-direction magic to help you make it through the day.

Quick View

- Sharing is a concept that's barely understood by a young child, so is it really fair to punish a child for not being able to do it?
- A better way to handle sharing is to apply a little redirecting magic, it's worth trying.

101. Compromise ~ Crucial for Relationships

Children live in the present moment. Because children live in the present, they feel like their disagreements have to be dealt with *right now!* That causes them to scream for a parent to come and deal with things *immediately,* especially when a sibling is involved. Most parents I know don't really enjoy that. Parents either scream, "Work it out!" or they appear on the scene as judge and jury all wrapped up in one.

Another option a parent can use is to become the facilitator. A facilitator doesn't ignore or take sides; he simply continues to ask questions, flushing out the concerns, until things are resolved to the satisfaction of both parties.

Because children have very little experience with compromise, they need to be taught how to resolve situations over and over again. Once the children understand how this process works, a parent can pull away and let them negotiate on their own.

Why not just punish? Because the way children resolve sibling issues teaches communication, resolution, fairness, and give and take—all valuable skills needed to become a successful adult.

This conversation shows you how to be totally neutral.

Mom: "Sam, what do you have to say about what happened? What do you wish could happen now?"

Mom: "Molly, What do you have to say about what happened? What do you wish could happen now?"

Mom: "Sam, can you give Molly what she wants? If not, why not?"

Mom: "Molly can you give Sam what he wants? If not, why not?"

Mom: "Sounds like neither one of you likes the idea the other one has. Since you've each heard what the other one has to say, it's time to give a little. What's one thing your sister has asked for that you could give her so you can work this out? What's one thing your brother has asked for that you could give him so you can work this out?"

The specifics will be different for each situation, but the children do all the work. The parent guides them, while taking a back seat in the discussion. By asking the same questions of both children, the parent conveys neutrality, and the siblings never feel as though the parent is taking a side.

The children say what's true for them without fear of punishment. They learn that compromise in relationships is not only possible, but also necessary, and can be done in a sweet respectful way. I think this is a great lesson to teach a child, one that will serve him/her for a lifetime.

Quick View

- Children have very little experience with compromise. The best way to teach compromise is for a parent to act as a facilitator and remain neutral. Once the siblings understand how this process works, parents can pull away and let them negotiate on their own.

- When children are free to express what's true for them without fear of punishment. They learn that compromise in relationships is not only possible, but also necessary.

102. Two Children ~ One Easy, One Difficult

When a parent has one easy and one difficult child, the parent naturally thinks he should be hard on the difficult child and a bit more lenient on the easy child. Choosing to do that may be attributed, in part, to feelings of guilt. The parent may feel that the difficult child is the way she is due to something the parent did or did not do.

Your child's temperament is *not* a reflection of your parenting. Both the easy and difficult children were born that way. You can't take credit for the easy child, and you shouldn't blame yourself for the difficult child either.

Make sure the rules are the same for all siblings, or the children may begin to feel that expectations are unfair. The easy child may feel like the bar is always set higher for him because you know he can do it. The difficult child may seem to enjoy that the bar is set a bit lower for her, but deep inside she feels hurt that you don't expect as much from her. She begins thinking, "Why bother trying? They don't expect me to reach that goal anyway."

Don't forget, the easy child leads by example, but so does the difficult child. The easy child shows the difficult child the benefits of behaving. The difficult child shows the easy child the pitfalls of misbehavior. The truth is that all of your children need the kind of compassion and love that only *you* can provide. Having one set of rules will allow you to accomplish that.

Quick View

- It doesn't matter if you have one easy child and one difficult child; the rules need to be the same for both.
- A benefit to having the same rules for all siblings is that the easy child leads by example, but so does the difficult child.

CHAPTER
15

TRAVEL

103. Technology ~ All I Get Is Bad News

Are you tired of only hearing about the bad news and misbehavior that occurred at home while you were in a meeting or on a plane? Don't get me wrong, hearing about any problems or misbehavior at home is important. It gives the stay-at-home parent a way to vent, which helps keep him or her sane, and keeps the working/traveling parent in the loop as well.

To avoid only hearing about bad news, consider setting up two email accounts instead of just one. Use one account for good news, and the other account for bad news and reports of misbehavior. This allows the working/traveling parent to decide which email account he or she wants to read first. More importantly it sends a message to the kids that nothing, good or bad, gets missed when a parent is working or traveling.

Another benefit to having two emails is that when the working/traveling parent does call in, the phone call can stay focused on love, fun and whatever family rituals you use to stay connected.

This can also work online as well. Just set up two Skype accounts or two FaceTime accounts. Since the working/traveling parent will be able to see which address the family is calling in on, the good news or bad news line, they're able to prepare before answering.

Quick View

- Set up two email accounts, or two Skype accounts. This keeps you connected, allows the stay-at-home parent to vent, and shows the kids that you're still involved, even though you're working or out of town.
- Don't forget that story time, baseball games, recitals or special events can be viewed online by turning the computer camera around.

104. Maps ~ Where in the World Is Mom?

Next time you go on a business trip, take a camera with you, a disposable if need be. Take a picture of you leaving the house, at the airport, on the plane, getting a rental car, at the hotel, in the meeting, and eating at a restaurant. When you get home use the photos as they are or turn them into magnets.

Post a map on the refrigerator and allow your child to use the photos to follow the traveling parent's trip. When Mom is at the airport, the child puts the photo of Mom on the area of the map where the airport is in your hometown. When Dad is on the plane, the child can move the photo across the country, and so on. This allows your child to see that the traveling parent is doing his or her job, and then coming back home. This also gives the traveling parent something to talk about on the phone.

Instead of buying expensive gifts for your children each time you travel, which can be difficult to find as you're rushing from meeting to plane, bring home little things to use for "show and tell" or craft projects. Bring home ticket stubs, postcards, pictures of historical things from each city, restaurant receipts, menus, nametags, things you can get at airports. Each night when you call, you can talk about the cool things you've picked up today. Doing this also makes it easier for the traveling parent to integrate back into the family when he or she gets home.

Quick View

- When my kids were little, their grandfather traveled around the world a lot. When he returned, he'd give the kids the different currency and other unusual trinkets. Those were the things the kids used at school for show and tell for years.

105. Planes ~ I'm Breaking My Own Rule

Taking a plane ride with a child can be a daunting task. There's nowhere to go to release pent up energy and no place for timeout, if that's something you normally do at home. Instead of saying, "Sit still and stop kicking the seat," for hours on end, here are a couple of ideas.

Go to the dollar store and purchase really small throw away toys for every half hour you'll be on the flight. Make sure to bring a small garbage bag for all the cardboard the toys are wrapped in, so you don't impact the flight attendant.

Or bring several electronic selections that your child hasn't seen to watch.

The key to making this work is to tell your child that she gets a toy or a video, if she stays in her seat and is somewhat quiet. If she gets loud or restless, you stop giving her toys for five minutes, or stop the video for five minutes. The toys/video, or the withholding of toys/video, becomes your timeout.

Sometimes, there's just no way to comfort a child on a plane, but this gives you a better shot at passing the time quietly.

Quick View

- Okay, I said bribing a child could backfire. And I still believe that. But a plane ride is just one of the exceptions! What can I say, I broke my own rule?

106. Re-Entry ~ A Game of Clue

Sometimes when a parent returns after a long day at work or a business trip, a child might pull away, be disrespectful or unco-operative, unconsciously attempting to punish you for being gone. The underlying reason for this is usually a fear that the parent wasn't coming back, despite all the reassurances to the contrary. If your child has a hard time with your re-entry give this a try.

Younger Children:

When leaving the office or after you've deplaned: Call home, using a hands free device, to begin the integration process.

10 minutes away: Call home to inform your child of how close you are to walking in the front door. Use familiar landmarks so she can picture where you are.

Pulling into the neighborhood: Call and ask her where she plans to greet you.

At home: Make your child your first priority until (s)he's comfortable and relaxed.

Older Children:

Clue—The ritual: When you're about 30 minutes from home, call and ask your child to give you one clue as to where (s)he'll be greeting you tonight.

Call every 10 minutes until you get home, even if you know where (s)he's hiding.

Quick View ———————————————

- These games allow kids to warm-up slowly, as you make your way home, instead of having to warm up instantly when you walk in the door.

107. Staying Connected ~ I Miss You

Some children just feel sad, or out of sorts when a parent travels. These tips will help remind kids that you're still a part of family life, even though you're traveling.

- Write short "Good Morning" notes for each of the days you'll be out of town.
- Skype or record yourself reading bedtime stories so your child hears your voice each night. Use a bell to let him know when it's time to turn the page.
- Give him a t-shirt that smells like you, so he feels connected to you. Spray cologne or perfume on it, if need be.
- Give your child an unbreakable "special" object to care for until you return. This sends the silent message, "I'll be home soon or I wouldn't have given this to you."
- Let kids tuck something special of theirs into a traveling parents suitcase.
- Stay connected by doing special projects. Younger kids can follow the progression of your trip on a map. Older kids can interview you about the cities you're visiting. Discuss history, famous landmarks, and capitols. Don't forget to bring back those fun mementos from the airport.

Quick View

- Give your child a "special" object or t-shirt to care for while you're gone.
- Use Skype or FaceTime to check in and continue family rituals.
- Spend 5-10 minutes each evening doing a "special project" with each child.
- Let the kids tuck something special of theirs into a traveling parents suitcase.

108. The End ~ Courage and Intuition

Many parents are afraid a time will come during their parenting years when they won't instinctively or immediately know what to do. I can promise you, it will happen, but you'll be able to handle it.

I'm convinced that everything you need to handle the job of parenting your child is already inside of you, including the ability to find answers when you need them. We all have something inside of us that tells us when we're on track, and lets us know if the information is right for us. It's called intuition.

All the information you needed to begin parenting began to flow the moment you held your child for the first time. Parenting isn't about always having to stay in control so you'll be ready to go when and if something happens. Parenting is about having faith that what you need will come into your mind the minute you need it.

Parenting information and research changes all the time. Don't let that confuse you. Use your intuition to see if what you've found is a match for you, your child and your family. Take all advice with a grain of salt, including mine, and if something doesn't ring true for you, don't use it. After you've tried a method in this book, followed the instructions as stated, and had success, make it your own. Use your own words so it sounds like you.

I hope this book has given you some new, conscious ways to look at parenting, and that these tips will allow you to respond instead of react. All you need to do is have the courage to make it from one moment to the next. The most important thing to do in parenting is to enjoy the parenting process. You will grow and change as much as your child grows and changes. Isn't that what life is all about? Happy parenting!

About the Author

Sharon Silver is an educator, author, powerful speaker, coach and TV and radio host. Her mission has always been to help parents focus on ways to respond, and set clear, loving boundaries instead of punish.

Sharon has always had an intuitive understanding of parenting. Her education is in Parenting and Early Childhood Development. She has a deep passion for the work of Magda Gerber, Arnold Gesell and T. Berry Brazelton, and has been a facilitator for The Cline/Fay Institute and The International Network for Children and Families.

Silver is the former host of *Stop Reacting and Start Responding* on MomTV.com and *HerInsight* radio. She can also be found at PopSugar.com in the parenting section, AskMoxie.org and ParentalWisdom.com.

Sharon's commitment to children and families resulted in her appearance on an episode of the *Oprah Winfrey Show* called, "Hitting, Spanking, Smacking: Should it happen to your child?"

Join her on social media @:

Website: www.proactiveparenting.net
Blog: http://proactiveparenting.net/category/blog
Facebook: www.facebook.com/ProactiveParentingTips
Twitter: Sharon_Silver
Look Sharon up on google+ as either Sharon Silver or Proactive Parenting.
Pinterest: http:www.pinterest.com/ProactiveParent/Boards
Bulk purchases: howard@proactiveparenting.net

More Tips, Bulk Orders and Speaking

More Tips

Proactive Parenting also offers articles, blogs, downloadable seminars and coaching support. To see what's available go to: www.proactiveparenting.net now.

To Stay in Touch

To learn more about current parenting techniques, parenting in general, and to receive articles from me and other Drs./educators, plus several free gifts, notices of special friends/family discounts and sales, and pre-registration opportunities for online events, sign up for our monthly newsletter by opting-in at: www.proactiveparenting.net

Speaking

To inquire about having Sharon Silver come speak at your school, or to host a *Lunch and Learn Parent Seminar* for your parent/employees like Intel, eBay, PayPal and other companies have, go to www.proactiveparenting.net and click on "speaking."

Bulk Orders

To inquire about discounts for bulk purchases of this book for your church, doctors office, school, cooperation or organization, or to use as a fundraiser for your non-profit, call the business office @ 415-937-2359.

Index

Index

Index

Specific Techniques:

CPSIA information can be obtained at www.ICGtesting.com
Printed in the USA
BVOW06s1226241215

430969BV00022B/72/P